BILL COSBY

BILL COSBY

Solomon J. Herbert
and
George H. Hill

Senior Consulting Editor
Nathan Irvin Huggins
Director
W.E.B. Du Bois Institute for Afro-American Research
Harvard University

CHELSEA HOUSE PUBLISHERS
New York   Philadelphia

AUG 1 6 2004

Chelsea House Publishers
Editor-in-Chief   Remmel Nunn
Managing Editor   Karyn Gullen Browne
Copy Chief   Juliann Barbato
Picture Editor   Adrian G. Allen
Art Director   Maria Epes
Deputy Copy Chief   Mark Rifkin
Assistant Art Director   Noreen Romano
Manufacturing Manager   Gerald Levine
Systems Manager   Lindsey Ottman
Production Manager   Joseph Romano
Production Coordinator   Marie Claire Cebrián

Black Americans of Achievement
Senior Editor   Richard Rennert

Staff for   BILL COSBY
Editorial Assistant   Michele Haddad
Picture Researcher   Alan Gottlieb
Designer   Ghila Krajzman
Cover Illustration   Patti Oleon

    5   7   9   8   6   4

Library of Congress Cataloging-in-Publication Data
Herbert, Solomon.
    Bill Cosby/by Solomon Herbert and George Hill.
       p.   cm.—(Black Americans of achievement)
    Includes bibliographical references and index.
    Summary: Examines the life and show business career of Bill Cosby.
    ISBN 0-7910-1121-6
         0-7910-1146-1 (pbk.)
    1. Cosby, Bill, 1937– —Juvenile literature.   2. Entertainers—
United States—Biography—Juvenile literature.   3. Comedians—
United States—Biography—Juvenile literature.   [1. Cosby, Bill,
1937– .   2. Entertainers.   3. Afro-Americans—Biography.]
I. Hill, George H.   II. Title.   III. Series.
PN2287.C632S65   1991
792.7′028′092—dc20   91-7373
[92]   CIP
[B]   AC

Frontispiece: *Bill Cosby relaxes
in his dressing room between
takes of "I Spy," the first
television series in which he
starred.*

CONTENTS

———— ❦ ————

On Achievement 7
Coretta Scott King

1
America's Favorite 11

2
"It Wasn't Always Easy" 21

3
Shorty's Struggles 31

4
"The Old School Try" 43

5
"A Very Funny Fellow" 53

6
Breaking New Ground 63

7
Branching Out 75

8
The King of Comedy 85

Appendix: A Bill Cosby Miscellany 96

Chronology 98

Further Reading 99

Index 100

BLACK AMERICANS OF ACHIEVEMENT

RALPH ABERNATHY
civil rights leader

MUHAMMAD ALI
heavyweight champion

RICHARD ALLEN
religious leader and social activist

LOUIS ARMSTRONG
musician

ARTHUR ASHE
tennis great

JOSEPHINE BAKER
entertainer

JAMES BALDWIN
author

BENJAMIN BANNEKER
scientist and mathematician

AMIRI BARAKA
poet and playwright

COUNT BASIE
bandleader and composer

ROMARE BEARDEN
artist

JAMES BECKWOURTH
frontiersman

MARY MCLEOD BETHUNE
educator

BLANCHE BRUCE
politician

RALPH BUNCHE
diplomat

GEORGE WASHINGTON CARVER
botanist

CHARLES CHESNUTT
author

BILL COSBY
entertainer

PAUL CUFFE
merchant and abolitionist

FATHER DIVINE
religious leader

FREDERICK DOUGLASS
abolitionist editor

CHARLES DREW
physician

W.E.B. DU BOIS
scholar and activist

PAUL LAURENCE DUNBAR
poet

KATHERINE DUNHAM
dancer and choreographer

MARIAN WRIGHT EDELMAN
civil rights leader and lawyer

DUKE ELLINGTON
bandleader and composer

RALPH ELLISON
author

JULIUS ERVING
basketball great

JAMES FARMER
civil rights leader

ELLA FITZGERALD
singer

MARCUS GARVEY
black-nationalist leader

DIZZY GILLESPIE
musician

PRINCE HALL
social reformer

W. C. HANDY
father of the blues

WILLIAM HASTIE
educator and politician

MATTHEW HENSON
explorer

CHESTER HIMES
author

BILLIE HOLIDAY
singer

JOHN HOPE
educator

LENA HORNE
entertainer

LANGSTON HUGHES
poet

ZORA NEALE HURSTON
author

JESSE JACKSON
civil rights leader and politician

JACK JOHNSON
heavyweight champion

JAMES WELDON JOHNSON
author

SCOTT JOPLIN
composer

BARBARA JORDAN
politician

MARTIN LUTHER KING, JR.
civil rights leader

ALAIN LOCKE
scholar and educator

JOE LOUIS
heavyweight champion

RONALD MCNAIR
astronaut

MALCOLM X
militant black leader

THURGOOD MARSHALL
Supreme Court justice

ELIJAH MUHAMMAD
religious leader

JESSE OWENS
champion athlete

CHARLIE PARKER
musician

GORDON PARKS
photographer

SIDNEY POITIER
actor

ADAM CLAYTON POWELL, JR.
political leader

LEONTYNE PRICE
opera singer

A. PHILIP RANDOLPH
labor leader

PAUL ROBESON
singer and actor

JACKIE ROBINSON
baseball great

BILL RUSSELL
basketball great

JOHN RUSSWURM
publisher

SOJOURNER TRUTH
antislavery activist

HARRIET TUBMAN
antislavery activist

NAT TURNER
slave revolt leader

DENMARK VESEY
slave revolt leader

MADAM C. J. WALKER
entrepreneur

BOOKER T. WASHINGTON
educator

HAROLD WASHINGTON
politician

WALTER WHITE
civil rights leader and author

RICHARD WRIGHT
author

ON ACHIEVEMENT

Coretta Scott King

BEFORE YOU BEGIN this book, I hope you will ask yourself what the word excellence means to you. I think that it's a question we should all ask, and keep asking as we grow older and change. Because the truest answer to it should never change. When you think of excellence, perhaps you think of success at work; or of becoming wealthy; or meeting the right person, getting married, and having a good family life.

Those important goals are worth striving for, but there is a better way to look at excellence. As Martin Luther King, Jr., said in one of his last sermons, "I want you to be first in love. I want you to be first in moral excellence. I want you to be first in generosity. If you want to be important, wonderful. If you want to be great, wonderful. But recognize that he who is greatest among you shall be your servant."

My husband, Martin Luther King, Jr., knew that the true meaning of achievement is service. When I met him, in 1952, he was already ordained as a Baptist preacher and was working towards a doctoral degree at Boston University. I was studying at the New England Conservatory and dreamed of accomplishments in music. We married a year later, and after I graduated the following year we moved to Montgomery, Alabama. We didn't know it then, but our notions of achievement were about to undergo a dramatic change.

You may have read or heard about what happened next. What began with the boycott of a local bus line grew into a national movement, and by the time he was assassinated in 1968 my husband had fashioned a black movement powerful enough to shatter forever the practice of racial segregation. What you may not have read about is where he got his method for resisting injustice without compromising his religious beliefs.

He adopted the strategy of nonviolence from a man of a different race, who lived in a distant country, and even practiced a different religion. The man was Mahatma Gandhi, the great leader of India, who devoted his life to serving humanity in the spirit of love and nonviolence. It was in these principles that Martin discovered his method for social reform. More than anything else, those two principles were the key to his achievements.

This book is about black Americans who served society through the excellence of their achievements. It forms a part of the rich history of black men and women in America—a history of stunning accomplishments in every field of human endeavor, from literature and art to science, industry, education, diplomacy, athletics, jurisprudence, even polar exploration.

Not all of the people in this history had the same ideals, but I think you will find something that all of them have in common. Like Martin Luther King, Jr., they all decided to become "drum majors" and serve humanity. In that principle—whether it was expressed in books, inventions, or song—they found something outside themselves to use as a goal and a guide. Something that showed them a way to serve others, instead of living only for themselves.

Reading the stories of these courageous men and women not only helps us discover the principles that we will use to guide our own lives but also teaches us about our black heritage and about America itself. It is crucial for us to know the heroes and heroines of our history and to realize that the price we paid in our struggle for equality in America was dear. But we must also understand that we have gotten as far as we have partly because America's democratic system and ideals made it possible.

We are still struggling with racism and prejudice. But the great men and women in this series are a tribute to the spirit of our democratic ideals and the system in which they have flourished. And that makes their stories special and worth knowing. ◆

BILL
COSBY

1

AMERICA'S FAVORITE

One of America's best-loved entertainers, Cosby has watched his popularity soar since "The Cosby Show" debuted on NBC in 1984. Among the chief reasons for the show's success have been his and costar Phylicia Rashad's (left) portrayal of people who are intelligent and comfortably middle class—making them very different from the stereotyped characters that most blacks have played on television.

BILL COSBY MIGHT never have emerged as one of television's most popular stars and a regular Thursday night fixture as Dr. Heathcliff Huxtable, all-American dad, were it not for his penchant for keeping late hours. It was during one of his forays into late-night television viewing that the inspiration for his top-rated "The Cosby Show" was born. The violence and vulgarity, not to mention the sexism and racism, that he saw on television that night seemed all too prevalent and deeply disturbed him.

"Over the years I'd seen an awful lot of the same kind of programs," Cosby said in 1983. "On detective programs everybody was driving down the block on two wheels, going through glass windows and dropping to their knees with a .357 Magnum. And the shows were rife with stereotypes. Anytime you saw a black actor or actress, you knew something negative was going to happen." A woman, he charged, was almost always portrayed as a scantily dressed plaything for the male hero; she was seldom, if ever, shown doing anything practical or demonstrating that she could get along in life without a man.

"Television is a fantastic medium that could very well be something, and should be something a family can look at and get a good feeling from," Cosby observed. "It should not be something that we feel afraid to turn on because it will grossly offend us or do a disservice to our children." So, Cosby began to kick around ideas for a new show. Creating a new television series, he said only half in jest, would be easier than throwing out his family's six television sets.

His first inclination was to develop a detective show that would have no guns, no violence, and no car chases. "I would solve crimes with my wits, as Columbo did, and my girl would be a strong woman with her own career," he explained. But the three major networks argued that such an offering would have no audience. There were simply too many private-eye and cops-and-robbers shows on the air at that time.

Cosby then hit on the idea of creating a show in which he would play a chauffeur who was married to a Hispanic plumber. After some urging from Cosby's wife, Camille, this idea evolved into a weekly half-hour comedy series depicting a black family headed by, of all things, a father *and* a mother who were articulate professionals. Cosby's new show would not be like television's other all-black situation comedies, which relied heavily on a string of one-liners, put-downs, and racial stereotypes for laughs. Instead, it would be a thoughtful, sensitive, intelligent series that piqued people's sense of humor about the daily absurdities of family life.

Cosby, in concert with Carsey-Werner, the production company established by television executives Marcy Carsey and Tom Werner, once again approached ABC, CBS, and NBC with his proposal. The first two networks nixed the concept. But this time, NBC's president, Grant Tinker, and its head of programming, Brandon Tartikoff, shared Cosby's vision and ordered seven episodes to be taped for the network's fall 1984 schedule.

According to Cosby, what sold them on the show was that Tartikoff had seen him on "The Tonight Show" doing a routine about his daughters and the

"I want to show a family that has a good life," Cosby said of the Huxtables, the closely knit clan that he heads on NBC's *"Cosby Show."* In developing the series, Cosby cast himself as Dr. Heathcliff Huxtable, an obstetrician; the other members of the family are (clockwise from left) Cliff's wife, Clair, a lawyer (played by Phylicia Rashad); and their five children: Sondra (Sabrina LeBeauf), Theo (Malcolm Jamal Warner), Vanessa (Tempestt Bledsoe), Rudy (Keshia Knight Pulliam), and (not shown) Denise (Lisa Bonet).

problems he was having with them. "Tartikoff obviously felt," Cosby said, "that there was enough amusing and educational material in the stories about my wife and children that I had been using for years in my nightclub act."

"The Cosby Show" premiered in September 1984 and was an instant runaway hit. By year's end, it had surged to the front of the ratings race, replacing Tom Selleck's "Magnum P.I." as television's number one program. "The Cosby Show" has remained at or near the top of the ratings ever since.

The mix of characters and the affection they hold for one another are obvious to the show's fans and are in large part responsible for "The Cosby Show"'s huge popularity with viewers of all ages. "When we were hiring the kids, we looked for that special quality which would project on-screen, a special harmony with each other like a real family," Cosby noted. "I don't mind working with everyone, because I knew from day one that this show was going to be me."

According to the series' younger stars, Cosby is very much like the television character he plays on the show: warm, understanding, and fun. Lisa Bonet, for instance, who is cast as Dr. Huxtable's fashionably punk daughter Denise, has nothing but words of praise for her boss: "Bill is real honest, and goes out of his way to help us, critiquing and complimenting our work."

Tempestt Bledsoe, who plays preppy Vanessa, the next-to-youngest daughter, is another admirer of Cosby's and sometimes even calls him Dad. "He can walk up to kids and start playing with them," she said. "And he can make kids behave without telling them to do so."

Malcolm Jamal Warner, another of Cosby's youthful television brood, was a case in point. He almost did not make it onto the cast because of the way he acted during his tryout. "When Malcolm Jamal Warner came in to audition for the role of my thirteen-year-old son Theo," Cosby mused, "he rolled his eyes and sucked his teeth to show disgust. I said to Malcolm, 'Son, if you were talking to your own father, would you do that?' Malcolm said, 'No, sir.' 'What would your father say?' 'He'd question my sanity.' "

Cosby then explained to Warner that what the show was attempting to do was unlike anything that had preceded it in the black situation comedy genre: " 'What this show is about is the love of a husband for his wife. It's about a man still courting his wife. It's about a wife's being sensitive to her love for her husband and all five of her children. It's about children who sometimes have their priorities in the wrong place but who respect their parents and can learn. It's about kids who are precocious but not nasty. It's about fun.' Malcolm got the point," Cosby said, "and has turned out to be a very fine young actor."

On one occasion, Warner said, "we were taping and Keshia Pulliam [who plays the youngest daughter, Rudy] came around a corner and bumped right into Mr. C. It was so sudden she started crying. Mr. C. stopped the taping for about five minutes, then said, 'Let's do it again.' But Keshia was still a little sad—so this time when she came around the corner Mr. C. got down on the floor and started crying. Keshia started laughing and felt a lot better."

According to Warner, Cosby is "kind but tough—and always funny. When I'm finally a father, I'd like to copy his style. He's very approachable. You can talk to him whether you're eight or eighty."

Another reason why "The Cosby Show" works so well can be attributed to the similarities between the on-screen Huxtable clan and Cosby's real-life family. In the show, Heathcliff Huxtable, an obstetrician, is married to Clair, a beautiful lawyer, and has five high-spirited children, four girls and a boy. Off-screen, Dr. William H. Cosby is happily married to Camille, with whom he has four daughters and a son.

"The character he's playing is very close to the real Bill Cosby," observed actor Robert Culp, who costarred with Cosby in his first television series, "I Spy," in the mid-1960s. "He's taken off all the veils." According to the late entertainer Sammy Davis, Jr., a longtime friend of the Cosbys', Clair is also a lot like Cosby's wife, Camille. "Bill [has] used a lot of 'Camillisms' in the show," Davis noted. "The woman who plays the part is not a carbon copy—as no one could be—but in terms of dignity and beauty and love in the home, she's like Camille."

As a result, the viewers of "The Cosby Show" are presented with a glimpse into Cosby's private life. Even the Manhattan town house in which the Huxtables live is a replica of the Cosbys' own home, right down to the Queen Anne chairs, upholstered wing chairs, case clock, Oriental rug, and Varnette Honeywood paintings. Cosby went so far as to hire Anita Kistlinger, the designer who decorated his New York City town house, to help create the look

A claim by Theo (Malcolm Jamal Warner) that receiving poor grades in school will not keep him from getting a good job prompts his father (Cosby) to give him an economics lesson on the series premiere of "The Cosby Show." In discussing episodes such as this one, Cosby said that "it would give me terrific satisfaction to be able to reach some of those kids who are kicking their lives around."

he wanted. This familiar forum has made it easier for him to present his innermost feelings and desires to the public.

And one of Cosby's most burning desires has long been to be an educator. "Teaching kids and providing a good example for them is very important, meaningful to me," he acknowledged in 1980. "I love being around them, and I feel I gain as much from them as they hopefully learn from me."

Harvard University professor Alvin Poussaint has been hired by Cosby to review "The Cosby Show"'s scripts and make sure that they do not contain any racially offensive material. "I won't deal with the foolishness of racial overtones," Cosby insisted. "The race situation is not funny, and I don't see jokes making it any better."

Phylicia Rashad, who plays Camille's counterpart on the show, has obviously felt the same way. She was flattered to be chosen for the part of Cosby's on-screen wife because she recognizes "The Cosby Show" for what it is: a way of presenting the television audience with excellent black role models. "Kids learn by example," she said, "and I think we're very good ones."

"The Cosby Show" has spawned some criticism from observers who feel that Cosby's vision of family life is not "black enough." Some of these critics have gone so far as to say that he has sold out, creating a blackface "Father Knows Best" (a popular 1950s television series that presented an artificially rosy outlook). Cosby has answered these charges by saying that his show is true to life because America certainly has middle-class black families, including ones in which the father is a doctor and the mother is a lawyer. "My point," Cosby said, "is that this is an American family—an *American* family—and if you want to live like they do, and you're willing to work, the opportunity is there."

Among the people who agree with Cosby's aim to uplift his race is Dr. Alvin Poussaint, the Harvard professor whom the television star hired to review "The Cosby Show"'s scripts and make sure they rang true, were culturally authentic, and were free of unintended insults. "Blacks are emerging on the screen," Poussaint said in 1985, "as decent, productive human beings—not the clowns they used to portray. It's a big step forward. [The] breakthrough is helping to change perceptions about blacks by both whites and blacks. It demonstrates that blacks have talent and can move up, and it cuts racial barriers by showing that we're all just people."

To Cosby, the latter point is the bottom line. "I believe the main reason our show is being watched all across the country," he said, "is because everybody—

black people, white people, Native Americans—is saying, 'You know, I have a kid who acts exactly like that.' It brings people together. This series is for me a love affair for all the years that I've been a well-paid entertainer. It's my way to say to the people who have enjoyed my works, 'I can do this, and here is a form of entertainment that I hope you will feel good about.' "

Cosby's work on the show has earned a shelf of prizes, including a Golden Globe Award, numerous People's Choice Awards, a CEBA (Communications Excellence to Black Audiences) Award, and a Humanitas Award. "The Cosby Show" has also won numerous Emmy Awards for being the Outstanding Comedy Series. (Having already won five Emmy Awards for performances earlier in his career, Cosby has asked to have his name removed from contention in the Best Actor category to allow his fellow actors a chance to receive some recognition.) Hoping to reap similar laurels, a number of other television series have tried to copy "The Cosby Show"'s proven formula. Yet the only series about middle-class blacks that has come close to rivaling the accomplishments of "The Cosby Show" is the highly rated "A Different World," of which Cosby is executive producer.

With all the accolades and honors bestowed on Bill Cosby, one might get the impression that everything came easily to him. But life for him has had its share of struggles, and his success has not come without a lot of hard work and sacrifice. Indeed, by following the bumpy road that has led to his recent triumphs, there are lessons to be learned. ◄◉►

2

"IT WASN'T ALWAYS EASY"

WILLIAM HENRY COSBY, Jr., was born at
3:00 A.M. on July 12, 1937, in North Philadelphia's
Germantown Hospital. His parents, William and
Anna Pearl Cosby, were childhood sweethearts from
Virginia who had migrated north during the Great
Depression in search of a better life. Bill was the first
of their four sons. His brothers, James, Russell, and
Robert, arrived, respectively, two, five, and nearly
nine years after Bill did.

During the earliest part of Bill's childhood, his
family was typically lower middle class. Although
money was never plentiful for the Cosbys and they
had no luxuries to speak of, there was always a roof
over their head, food on the table, and a warm place
to sleep. As the clan began to grow, however, the
pressure of being the Cosbys' sole breadwinner took

*A gathering of youths in front of the Richard Allen Homes, the
low-income housing project in Philadelphia where Cosby grew up.
Cosby later said that during his boyhood years, "My family was
receiving welfare and public assistance, and we really needed
it—without it, my parents might not have been able to clothe us.
We would have had to beg."*

its toll on Bill's father, a former seminary student turned welder. Because welding jobs were in short supply, he took on all sorts of odd jobs to try to make ends meet, but he was unable to find enough work to support his wife and sons. Before long, he sought refuge in the bottle.

As his drinking became more chronic, the senior Cosby would wander off for days and weeks at a time. "My father," Bill, Jr., recalled years later, "left home many times. He would leave when the rent was due, or come home penniless on payday, swearing to my mother that he'd been robbed, and leave again. Once he vanished just before Christmas and we didn't have a cent."

On that occasion, Bill tried to cheer up his family by painting an orange crate with watercolors and then putting on top of it a Santa Claus figure that lit up. "When my mother saw it—about nine P.M. on Christmas Eve," according to Cosby, "she put on her coat and went out. She must have borrowed money from neighbors, but she came back with a kind of scrawny Christmas tree, and the next morning we all had a few little presents. We never really knew what it was like to have a father. The word still spells 'disappointment' to my brothers and me."

Eventually, the Cosbys had to move to where the rent was lower. They wound up crammed into a tiny two-bedroom apartment in the Richard Allen Homes, a low-income housing project in a poor black section of Philadelphia known as the Jungle. The screeching of metal wheels echoed through the barracks-like apartment buildings that lined the neighborhood's cobblestone streets as trains rumbled along the nearby elevated railway all day and night. According to Cosby, "When Mother would hang clothes the trains would go by and dirty them. But it wasn't a life of poverty. We had plenty of hot water and heat."

Bill shared a bed with his brother James, who had always been sickly. In 1945, however, James died from rheumatic fever. Shortly thereafter, William, Sr., joined the U.S. Navy and became a mess steward, leaving Bill in charge as "the man of the house." He seldom saw the elder Cosby after that, only when he returned to port for brief visits before shipping out again. The checks he sent back home helped pay the bills, but soon they stopped coming, and so did he.

Bill's mother went to work, toiling 12 hours a day as a maid to help feed and clothe her children, while Bill pitched in after school, hitting the streets with the shoeshine kit he fashioned out of empty orange crates. He roamed the downtown district, where people could afford to have their shoes shined, in an effort to earn pocket money that he added to the family kitty. "Bill was my everything," Anna Cosby said. "He was father, mother, brother and sister. . . . He was a big help to me."

Bill's affection for his mother, a tiny woman with a lilting laugh, was no less ardent. "There are many beautiful things about my mother," he has stated, "but the most beautiful is that she has never lost her femininity. She never became mother and father." Every night, she would tuck Bill and his brothers into bed and read aloud from Mark Twain and Jonathan Swift, the brothers Grimm and the Bible. Her relentless outpouring of love and devotion helped to smooth over poverty's rough edges.

One of the most satisfying moments in his life, Bill Cosby recounted in 1985, was when he had become successful enough "to walk into our home and say to my mother, 'You will never scrub any more floors or work in anybody else's house.'" Indeed, many years after he had become a multimillionaire, someone asked him where he found the energy to continue working so hard. "I think one of the most important things to understand," he said, "is that my mother, as a domestic, worked 12 hours a day, and then she would do the laundry, and cook the meals and serve them and clean, and for this she got $7 a day. So 12 hours a day of whatever I do is . . . easy."

Along with his mother, Bill's maternal grandfather, Samuel Russell, loomed as the major role model in his life. "He loved to tell stories that had some moral point about getting an education, working hard," Cosby recalled, "but you'd hardly notice because he'd be so funny and ramble around so much." It was at his grandfather's urging that Bill began to hone his own storytelling skills. At the end of each storytelling session, Samuel Russell would fish a quarter from a sock full of change that hung from his belt and reward his eldest grandson. Bill was beginning to learn that comedy could pay.

At this point in Bill's life, however, it still did not pay well enough. So Bill spent the summer of 1948, when he turned 11, clerking at a grocery store. He worked from six o'clock in the morning until six o'clock at night—and until nine o'clock on Saturdays—for eight dollars a week. When he returned to the racially mixed Mary Channing Wister Elementary School that fall, he took on another job. At the crack of dawn, he would head over to Marshall Street to sell fruit before reporting for classes. In the evenings, he would don the mantles of referee, peacemaker, taskmaster, and, when necessary, enforcer as he tried to keep his brothers in line until their mother came home from work.

Throughout these years, Christmastime for the Cosbys continued to exemplify just how hard their life was. Their apartment continued to lack a Christmas tree, festively wrapped presents, and stockings hung on a mantel. "We didn't have enough socks for our feet," Cosby remembered, "let alone any spare ones to hang." The Cosby boys would "celebrate"

Christmas Eve by sitting at the kitchen table without their mother, who had to spend the holiday working.

Bill Cosby harbors no bitterness about those difficult growing-up years. "Unhappiness should make a person appreciate happiness more, and hard times should hopefully give a person backbone and moral strength," he says. He has admitted, however, to having an obsession with staying out of debt because he spent much of his youth being hounded by bill collectors who were looking for payments his family simply did not have.

Despite the hardships they faced, the Cosby home was never a place of gloom and despair. For Bill, the radio became one of life's bright spots. "You had 'The Lone Ranger,' 'The Shadow,' 'Lights Out' and 'Inner Sanctum,'" he told the *Los Angeles Times*

Cosby shares a laugh with his maternal grandfather, Samuel Russell, on the porch of the latter's house in Philadelphia. Cosby credits his grandfather with being the first person to encourage him to develop his storytelling gifts.

According to Cosby, his mother, Anna, *"is the most unselfish being I've ever known. Many's the time I saw her come home from work exhausted and hungry—and give her supper to one of my brothers who was still hungry after he'd eaten his own."*

in 1989, listing a few of his favorite radio programs, "but I always listened for the comedy: Jack Benny, Burns and Allen, Jimmy Durante, Fred Allen. . . . When comedy was on, I was just happy to be alive."

Just as important in helping Bill retain an upbeat view of things was his mother's ability to maintain a sense of humor in the face of life's disappointments. "She would tell me that if I swallowed the seeds along with the grapes, branches would grow out of my ears and the neighbors would hang laundry on them," he recalled. "She would warn that if I kept playing with my navel, it was going to pop out and all of the air would spew out of my body and I'd fly around backwards, flopping around the room."

Anna Cosby's off-center humor obviously had a lasting effect on young Bill. For one thing, he learned at an early age to use his wit and humor to charm his mother. Sometimes, Bill would cajole a special treat out of her by reprising a humorous radio show he had heard earlier. "I'm a con man," he admitted years later. "That's how I started out to be a comedian . . . you start out at about three or four, conning your mother out of a cookie. You know she'll say no the first time you ask, but you also know that if you can get her to laughing, you can get around her."

"Bill could turn painful situations around and make them funny," added brother Robert. "You laughed to keep from crying." Bill, for example, liked to entertain his brothers in the kitchen. After volunteering to cook for the family to help ease his mother's work load, he would add dashes of food coloring to his breakfast offerings and make his brothers purple waffles and green scrambled eggs.

According to school pal Joe Johnson, "Bill's zany humor and clowning were his only weapons against the pain and heartache of living in the ghetto. Times were pretty bad for Bill, his mom and brothers. They were dogged by poverty."

As a result, much of the material Bill Cosby has used in his stand-up comedy repertoire, in his best-selling records and books, and on "The Cosby Show" is based on the 14 years of "Jungle" warfare he experienced while growing up in North Philadelphia. His routines about bunking with his bed-wetting brother Russell and fighting over who would sleep on the damp spot and about growing up thinking his name was Jesus Christ and another brother's name was Lookdammit are both derived from his boyhood days. "Addressing the two of us, my father would say, 'Lookdammit, stop jumping on the furniture! Jesus

Christ, can't you ever be still?' " Cosby wrote in *Fatherhood*.

Bill's father has remained the focus of much of his eldest son's comedy, which tends to paint the senior Cosby in a sympathetic light. Bill has joked about his father, whom he and his brothers called the Giant, stumbling home after a long night of drinking, then struggling to undress. The boys would listen for his pants to hit the floor. And if they heard a loud clink, they knew he still had some coins left in his pockets.

According to Matt Robinson, one of Cosby's oldest friends and a writer for "The Cosby Show," "We both came from the same background in Philadelphia, and few people understand the importance of that background in Bill's development as a story-teller and performer. Bill's sources of material not only come from his own family but from all the families he grew up with in Philadelphia. Because there wasn't much formal entertainment, like movies or theater, in our neighborhoods, we entertained ourselves. On porches and in backyards, we told the funny things that happened to us at home. Bill sopped it all up like a sponge."

"When I was a kid," wrote Cosby, "I always used to pay attention to things that other people didn't even think about. I'd remember funny happenings, just little trivial things, and then tell stories about them later. I found I could make people laugh, and I enjoyed doing it because it gave me a sense of security. I thought that if people laughed at what you said, that meant they liked you. Telling funny stories became, for me, a way of making friends."

Bill also plied his considerable wit outside the family to compensate for the two qualities in which he was sorely lacking: height (he was very short as a youngster) and academic prowess (he was a poor student in grade school). His cleverness often saved him from the bodily harm that someone a head taller might otherwise have inflicted on him in Philadelphia's tougher neighborhoods. "One time," recalled an old running buddy, "we ran into a bunch of dudes down the street hellbent on bouncing our heads on the sidewalk. Old Shorty walks right up to the leader and starts telling this guy how he'd been sent by the Salvation Army to tell all the kids in the neighborhood that there was free ice cream being given away, and if he wanted some he'd better hurry. The guys took off."

Bill's antics, however, never helped put a passing grade on his report card. If anything, they got in the way. "William would rather be a clown than a student and feels it is his mission to amuse classmates in and out of school," noted Mary Forchic, his sixth-grade teacher. "He is affable with a personality most pleasing and he tries to get by on that."

Bill Cosby was destined to learn the hard way that being funny was only part of what he needed to make it in life. ❧

3

SHORTY'S STRUGGLES

IF BILL COSBY had been graded solely on his athletic feats on the streets and school-yard courts of North Philadelphia, he would surely have been a straight-A student. He excelled in football, baseball, and basketball, and when he was not trying to make his friends laugh, he was dazzling them with his fluid moves, lightning speed, and physical dexterity. He was active in Police Athletic League competition and eventually became an outstanding pitcher and the captain of both his high school football and track teams.

Cosby was unquestionably bright. In academics, however, he was a dedicated underachiever, and he received a slew of dreadful report cards to prove it. At one time, he framed a selection of the worst ones and hung them on a wall. Included among them was the report card from Mary Forchic with her comments about his tendency to favor clowning over studying. She presided over a class at the Wister Elementary School for so-called unreachable sixth-grade students.

Despite the relatively brief amount of time Cosby spent in Forchic's class, she was to have a profound effect on his life. Unlike many of her contemporaries, who were content to baby-sit these troubled youngsters before passing them and their problems on to

Posing on the Temple University campus in his varsity-letter sweater, Cosby has come a long way from his boyhood days, when, he said, "we used to wad up newspapers and put 'em inside our sweaters to look like shoulder pads."

someone else, Forchic believed that any child could be reached with hard work, patience, and a generous portion of love thrown in for good measure. Forchic offered what behavioral scientists call positive reinforcement in working with her charges, often rewarding them with prizes, toys, and after-school snacks at a nearby soda fountain.

The first time Cosby ever ventured outside his own community was when Forchic treated him to a movie. "I was so happy to be downtown," he recalled. "After the movie, my teacher took me to dinner and then she rode me home in a taxicab. This was a big thing because in my neighborhood if you rode in a taxicab, something bad or something wonderful had happened to you."

In Forchic's opinion, "Every child is interested in something. The teacher's job is to find out what that something is. If it's baseball or football, for example, you can build math around that." For Cosby, it turned out to be performing in front of others, which led Forchic to cast him in a number of school plays. Cosby has since credited his sixth-grade teacher with giving him the initial nudge that started him down the road to becoming a professional entertainer. "Those classroom shows," he acknowledged, "were the things that generated the spark that said, 'Hey man, show biz feels good!' "

Forchic was also the person who inspired Cosby to become an educator. When he first entered her class, his report card was awash with U's (Unsatisfactory) and S's (Satisfactory); he received no O's (Outstanding). To go along with his other talents, Cosby was a master of excuses. He concocted wildly unbelievable stories about why he had not turned in his homework or completed his assignments. Forchic was so annoyed by one of his absurd excuses that she wrote on one report card, "William should either become a lawyer or an actor because he lies so well."

On occasion, he even went so far as to forge his mother's signature on his report card.

By the time Cosby moved on to the seventh grade, his card had no U's, only 6 S's, and 14 O's. "I worked Bill to death," Forchic recalled, "and the more I worked him, the better he was." Unfortunately, as soon as Cosby was outside her sphere of influence, he slipped back into his former bad habits, and his grades plummeted. Reminiscing about those childhood experiences, he said, "I was a con man. I found if I got people laughing, I could con along on the work."

When Cosby graduated from grade school into junior high school, Forchic told him, "You're a very intelligent young man, but you should be working at it." Her advice fell on deaf ears. "I refused to accept the responsibility," he admitted later. "I don't know what I even had in mind: it wasn't that I was going to be a professional football player or professional baseball player, or an artist or a drummer—it's just that I wanted to play."

Cosby continued his antics in junior high school, and sometimes, no matter how hard he tried, he could not avoid getting into a scrape or two. For the most part, though, he maneuvered his way past the hazards and pitfalls—truancy, alcohol abuse, and petty crime—that plagued many other inner-city youths. The reason he steered clear of trouble, Cosby said later, was mainly because he did not want to disappoint his mother: "The thing that always turned me around and kept me from taking a pistol and holding up a store or jumping in and beating some old person on the street was that I could go to jail, and this would bring a great amount of shame on my mother."

Despite his poor academic record in junior high school, Cosby scored very high on an IQ test, which put him in line to attend Philadelphia's Central

High, an all-boys school and among the top public high schools in the city. (His reputation as an excellent athlete, including his junior high record as captain of the tumbling team, did not hurt his chances.) All he needed to qualify for admission was to score well on the entrance exam and to get the endorsement of his junior high teachers. Cosby passed the test with flying colors. Then, armed with several letters of recommendation from his former teachers, he applied for admission and was accepted.

By the time Cosby arrived at Central High, he had outgrown his nickname, Shorty, having soared to nearly six feet tall. No longer undersized, he joined the football team—and learned to approach the sport in a far different manner from the way he and his buddies were accustomed to playing it on the streets of North Philadelphia. There, he said in his comedy routines, elaborately executed plays included everything from cutting behind black Chevys to waiting in living rooms. "Cosby," he claimed the quarterback would tell him in the huddle, "you go down to Third Street. Catch the J bus. Have them open the doors at Nineteenth Street. I'll fake it to you." The scenario would end with Cosby hopping off the bus just in time to catch a touchdown pass.

Cosby showed little interest in hitting the books, however; he could not find any motivation to study. So he fell back on his class-clown act. One day, for example, he was sitting in a classroom, reading a comic book instead of his textbook. The teacher took away the comic book and, with much disdain, admonished Cosby in front of the entire class. "You'll get this back at the end of the school year," the teacher said. "Why?" Cosby quipped. "Does it take you that long to read it?"

For the most part, Cosby found the members of the mostly white Central High student body to be snobs who refused to accept him because of his

While attending Temple University, Cosby was a fullback on the football team and the school's top performer in track and field. At most meets, he competed not only in the high jump—his best event—but in the long jump, the low hurdles, and the discus.

humble background. Feeling isolated and failing his classes, he did not take long to decide that the time had come for a change of scenery. Certainly, he could fare no worse at the more racially balanced, coeducational Germantown High School in North Philadelphia, where he would at least be around some familiar faces from his neighborhood.

Cosby was an instant success at Germantown— when it came to playing sports. He quickly established himself as the school's star athlete and became captain of the football and track teams. According to one fellow student, Cosby was also incredibly popular with the females. "Before the track meets he would entertain the girls with his stories and his jokes," Andrew Patterson told an interviewer. "I remember one time several girls tackled Bill, dragged him into the girls' room and smeared him with lipstick. Bill came out just grinning from ear to ear!"

But sports and the accolades they brought Cosby were not enough to carry him through high school. Neither was his class-clown routine. "I found that making people laugh was one way of getting attention," Cosby said, "so I concentrated on that. But it cost a lot." He was left back twice in the 10th grade before he made it into the 11th grade. By then, he was a senior citizen by high school standards and past the age limit for competing in city track meets. "I would have been twenty-one," he noted, "if I stayed to graduate from high school."

Instead, much to his mother's distress, Cosby chose to drop out of school in 1956 and get a job. His efforts to find employment in Philadelphia hardly proved successful. He worked briefly at a muffler plant and was hired as a shoe repairman's apprentice, but that job was short-lived as well. His employer fired him after failing to see any humor in the way Cosby sought to amuse himself: by nailing high heels onto men's shoes.

Cosby shined shoes for a while, then decided to give academics another try. This time, he attended night school. Yet he was still too restless to apply himself to his schoolwork. So, on one of the few occasions that he followed an example set by his father, he sought refuge from his troubles by joining the U.S. Navy in 1956.

"By the time I had made all my mistakes, quitting school and not paying attention to the people who told me to stick with it, I went into the service out of embarrassment," Cosby said. "The truth is, I'd just grown very tired of myself and thought perhaps there was a career for me in the service. If you stayed in for 20 years, you knew at least you'd get a certain amount of money for the rest of your life."

It took Cosby just a few days to realize that he had made a big mistake in joining the navy. "In boot camp," he recalled, "the force and the discipline were devastating to me. For the first time, I wasn't able to argue or make an excuse for why I didn't do something." Nevertheless, he settled into the basic training routine at the U.S. Marine Corps base in Quantico, Virginia, where he was schooled as a physical therapist.

Cosby was eventually assigned to the physical therapy unit at Bethesda Naval Hospital in Maryland. The Korean War had ended a few years earlier, and he spent his time as a physical therapist helping to rehabilitate war veterans, many of whom had been seriously injured during the conflict in Southeast Asia. He also went aboard ship with this unit and sailed from Newfoundland, Canada, to Guantánamo Bay, Cuba.

Cosby was stationed as well at the Philadelphia Naval Hospital, where he encountered a pilot who had lost an arm and an eye when his jet had crashed. "I wondered what my life would be like if I had no eyes, or was a quadriplegic," Cosby recalled. While helping those who were ill or handicapped to exercise, Cosby soon appreciated how lucky he was to have all his faculties intact.

But that was not all he discovered. "I met a lot of guys in the Navy," Cosby said, "who didn't have as much upstairs as I knew I did, yet here they were struggling away for an education. I finally realized I was committing a sin—a mental sin."

For the unfocused high school dropout, the realization that he was not getting the most out of his abilities became a turning point in his life. "That," Cosby said, "was when I decided to become something—stop fighting things I couldn't change and use the intelligence I was born with." He enrolled in a correspondence course to complete his high school education. When he passed the high school equivalency exam at the end of the course, he finally earned the treasured diploma that had eluded him for so long.

By then, Cosby's four-year enlistment was drawing to a close, and he was determined to further his education as soon as he got out of the military. His financial situation had not improved very much during his time in the navy, however. If he was to go to college, the school would have to be close to home so he could cut down on his expenses by living with his mother. He also knew that a scholarship was the only way he could afford a college education, and his only chance at winning such a scholarship was through athletics.

Nearing the age of 23, Cosby was finally ready to devote whatever time and energy attaining an education would require. But the question remained: Was anyone willing to give him the chance?

Fortunately for Cosby, he had continued to hone his athletic skills during his stint in the military by becoming a member of the U.S. Navy track team. He excelled in the 220-yard low hurdles, the discus, and the javelin. He also ran the 100-yard dash in a fleet-footed 10.2 seconds. But his star shone brightest in the high jump, where his personal best was an impressive 6 feet, 5 inches—a distance he reached at the national Amateur Athletics Union competition as a representative of the navy squad.

By 1960, when Cosby was ready to muster out of the navy, he had all the qualities that university athletic directors look for when recruiting. Not only was he a gifted athlete, but he was more mature, a lot hungrier, and significantly more serious about getting an education than most of the other prospective students were. Accordingly, he began to search for a college recruiter who appreciated these qualities.

He did not have to look very far. At one of the track meets Cosby attended as a member of the navy team, he met Gavin White, coach of both the track and football teams at Temple University in Philadelphia. White offered Cosby a full-tuition athletic scholarship, and in 1961 he enrolled at Temple as a physical education major.

Cosby joined the university's freshman basketball team and played fullback for the football squad. (Emlen Tunnell, a former professional football player and a scout for the Green Bay Packers and the New York Giants, rated Cosby a potential pro.) But track and field remained the Philadelphia native's best sport. Cosby became the Middle Atlantic Conference's high-jump champion and scored consistently high at meets because of his ability to compete in several different events.

At Temple, Cosby followed a hectic routine. In addition to the many practices, games, and meets he attended, he had to take on a number of part-time jobs, including working as a lifeguard at a municipal pool, to help support himself. Even so, he made no excuses. Changing his previous behavior, he paid attention to his studies this time and maintained a B

Temple University football and track coach Gavin White cited Cosby as both a team leader and a great joker who enjoyed "keeping the guys loosened up."

average. "I was reading, writing, challenging, exploring," he recalled. "I was secure in knowing I'd graduate and had my act together."

Cosby knew he had little choice except to study hard. "If I didn't make good at Temple," he said, "I knew what waited for me was a lifetime as a busboy or factory hand. I was so afraid that I made myself do well. On an evening when all I wanted was to go out with the boys, the specter of what might happen to me reared up, and boom, I was right back in my room studying."

Cosby at Temple University, about the time he left the school to pursue a career as a stand-up comic. "I must admit I was nervous in the beginning," he said, "but the experience has really been great for me. I know it's hard to keep pushing yourself into different areas, but you have to if you want to be around in a few years."

Although Cosby was decidedly more serious about his studies than he had ever been before and was a fierce competitor when it came to sports, he had by no means lost his sense of humor. He was, in fact, the team jokester, responsible for "keeping the guys loosened up," remembered Coach White.

On one occasion, Cosby was scheduled to run the final leg of a relay race for Temple in an important track meet at Philadelphia's Franklin Field. More than 60,000 fans stood and cheered as the starter fired his gun and the runners began to dash around the track. Cosby anxiously awaited his turn to perform for the crowd as his teammates passed the baton once, and then again, before handing it over to him for the anchor leg.

"We're all lined up there, with itchy feet, waiting to get the baton and take off," Cosby recalled. "But as my man gets near to the passing point, the baton hits his leg and flies up in the air. What does this cat do? He just starts to laugh. All the other anchor men are off and running, and I'm standing there waiting for this nut to stop laughing, pick up the baton, and give it to me. Finally, he retrieves it and walks over to me with the damn thing. Walks! I took it and bopped him right on the head with it, which is when the fans began screaming with laughter."

That was not all that happened, according to Cosby: "Old Cosby's a team player to the end, and I take off after those runners like a madman. I'm running and running, and passing one guy and then another, and then I get what you call rigor mortis if you're a runner. It's from the effort. First my face muscles freeze and then my chest, then my legs. I fall down, a beaten man if ever there was one, and while I'm down, the cat I had hit over the head comes up, takes the baton, and bops me back with it."

4

"THE OLD SCHOOL TRY"

BILL COSBY BEGAN spinning anecdotes into a comedy routine during his sophomore year at Temple University, while he was working part-time as a bartender in a downstairs saloon called the Underground. There, he often found himself telling amusing stories to the patrons. "When I went to work as a bartender to help with school," he said later, "I understood that if people enjoy conversation with the bartender, they leave tips. So I began collecting jokes, and learning how to work them up, stretch them out. For as long as you have the joke, you know you have the security that people will laugh."

Cosby soon became known for a repertoire of sidesplitting anecdotes that he shared with his customers. He learned quickly that the more he made his clients laugh, the bigger tips they gave him. And they laughed often. It was not long before the Underground's management asked Cosby to fill in for its resident comedian when the latter failed to show up for work.

Cosby eventually began to wonder if he could earn a living by telling jokes. He tested the waters next door at the Cellar, another subterranean bistro run by the owners of the Underground. He was billed as a stand-up comic, but that proved to be an

In his early years on the nightclub circuit, Cosby was labeled as a Negro comedian. As he described it, "I didn't have to trade on my being a Negro to succeed. I feel that I have no right to speak for all Negroes any more than a Jewish comedian can speak for all Jews. . . . I still speak out for equal rights, but I do it as an American, not as an entertainer."

inaccurate description. The Cellar did not have a stage; in order to be seen, Cosby had to perform perched atop a table. But the ceiling was not high enough to allow him to stand on the table, so he performed while sitting in a chair.

After a while, Cosby decided to get some guidance from his cousin Del Shields, the first black to host a television program in the Philadelphia area. Shields, who knew all about the different clubs that hired comics, helped Cosby land a series of local bookings. Occasionally, Cosby was even invited by Shields to warm up the audience before one of his television broadcasts, thus providing the budding young comic with an excellent opportunity to try out some new material.

Encouraged by the audiences' response, Cosby became a serious student of comedy, pouring over performances by some of the more notable comics of the day, such as Mel Brooks, Bob Newhart, and Jonathan Winters. He culled bits and pieces from their routines and incorporated them into his act while he searched for a style that he could call his own.

By the time winter break from college rolled around in 1962, Cosby decided to try his luck in New York City. Establishing himself in Philadelphia was one thing, but making a name for himself in the Big Apple, where there were a lot of young comics—including Allen Konigsberg and Joanie Molinsky, later known as Woody Allen and Joan Rivers—would be a real challenge. And to manage that, Cosby realized, "I had to work in places with a little more class."

He soon found just the right spot, landing a gig at the Gaslight, a Greenwich Village coffeehouse. For his efforts, the struggling young comedian was paid what he felt was an astronomically high salary: $60 a

According to Cosby, a stand-up comic can be called successful when "your stuff becomes funny because you are delivering it. You're a talking cartoonist, painting images in the audience's head."

week, plus a place to stay for free. What's more, the club's owner, Clarence Hood, immediately became one of the young comic's biggest boosters. "He believed in me when no one else did, when I was just a gawky kid with green sticking out all over," Cosby recalled in 1967. "You look around at these United States and you see how much racial conflict there is, but then you know there are people who can rise above all that, and respond to each other—human being to human being. Mr. Hood is a white, elderly gentleman from Mississippi and one of the truest people who ever lived. He looked after me and encouraged me to hope without a thought of what I could do for him."

Cosby continued to perform at the Gaslight after the new semester began. Somehow, he managed to juggle his schedule so that he could attend school during the day, travel to New York for a nighttime set or two at the club, and then return to Philadelphia for his classes and sports activities. He went through the remainder of the semester at this breakneck pace. When his summer vacation finally arrived, he took a breather from his schoolwork and concentrated full-time on his comedy gig at the Gaslight.

In his act, Cosby occasionally talked about his personal experiences. Nevertheless, most of his early comedy routines consisted of what he called "socio-political material." Like Godfrey Cambridge and Dick Gregory, the latter perhaps the most popular black comic in the early 1960s, Cosby drew heavily on the racial unrest that plagued America by poking fun at the tense relations between blacks and whites.

Around this time, Cosby signed with an agent, Roy Silver, among whose clients had been a young singer named Bob Dylan. After each performance, Cosby and Silver would scrutinize the 25-year-old comic's routines, which they had recorded, and try to figure out what jokes worked and why. They would

Dick Gregory was the leading black stand-up comic when Cosby broke into show business in the early 1960s. "I found that, to be a success, I'd have to jump over Dick Gregory," Cosby said. "I had the shadow of Gregory in everything I did."

listen to the tapes over and over until they had determined the best way for Cosby to deliver his lines.

In addition to studying his own technique, Cosby worked to perfect his craft by observing other comics during their performances at nearby Greenwich Village clubs. Chief among these comedians was the irreverent Lenny Bruce, whom Cosby saw repeatedly at the Village Vanguard. "I learned from Lenny," he said later, "that you could tell the truth onstage."

Accordingly, Cosby began to favor spinning lengthy stories about a variety of topics rather than serve up one-liners about race relations. He had never particularly enjoyed making light of racial matters, even though that was what most black comics were expected to do. "Racial humor was about 35 percent of my act when I first started," Cosby said. "But I realized that it was a crutch. What brought it home was when another comedian said to me, 'If you changed color tomorrow, you wouldn't have any material.' He meant it as a put-down, but I took it as a challenge."

Cosby then went out of his way to avoid telling hard-edged jokes whose barbs might offend part of his audience. To be confrontational simply was not his style. "I don't think you can bring the races together by joking about the differences between them," he said. "I'd rather talk about the similarities, about what's universal in their experiences."

Cosby did not have an easy time in making this transition, however. He had not yet perfected his ability to talk comically about the things he observed in everyday life, and the audiences would let him know it. Indeed, Cosby learned early in his career that a comedian's success depends in large part on his ability to win over the audience. It becomes much easier for a comic to perform, he noted, when the audience believes what he says next will be funny. "If

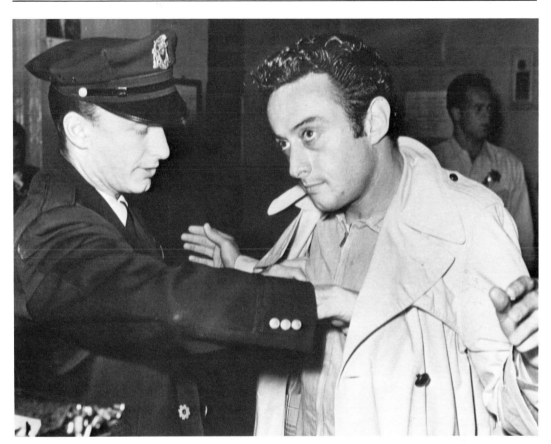

the audience knows you can be funny when you want to be," he said, "they will be willing to wait for that payoff."

For the most part, Cosby's efforts to improve his act paid off handsomely, especially after a review of his Gaslight show appeared in the *New York Times*. "His viewpoint is fresh, slightly ironic, and his best quips are extremely funny," wrote critic Paul Gardner. After that rave, crowds began flocking to the club to catch Cosby's act. His engagement at the Gaslight was extended, and his salary was upped to $175 a week.

By summer's end, Cosby had landed a gig at Chicago's Gate of Horn for $200 a week. He finished the engagement just in time to race back to school

Lenny Bruce, one of Cosby's comic idols, is arrested in 1961 for allegedly using obscene language in his nightclub act. Watching Bruce perform his uniquely controversial material inspired Cosby to abandon jokes about the race situation and to establish his own brand of humor instead.

and report for preseason football practice. He tried hard to keep up with his studies and fulfill his commitment to the Temple athletic department while working at night as a comic. But when Philadelphia's Town Hall offered Cosby the opportunity to perform for $250 a night, he found himself caught in a conflict. Accepting the gig, he realized, would prevent him from accompanying the football team on an overnight trip to a game in Ohio.

To make matters worse, Temple staff member George Makris warned Cosby that he would be kicked off the squad if he did not travel with the team. After much soul-searching, Cosby elected to leave school in favor of pursuing a career as a stand-up comic. It was, he said later, the toughest decision he ever had to make.

Perhaps worst of all, Cosby's decision to withdraw from Temple left his mother heartbroken. "When Bill quit college I was so unhappy it made me ill," she recalled. "For six weeks I walked back and forth, from room to room, asking myself, 'Why? Why?' When you haven't finished school yourself and your child turns down a chance for a college degree, it's a terrible experience."

Cosby, however, was determined to make it as an entertainer, and he forged ahead. "Once I decided it was a way to make a living, the struggle was on," he said. "Breaking into show business is one of the hardest . . . longest . . . most discouraging things you can do. If you want to make the old school try, you better have plenty of guts and determination, 'cause you'll need all you can muster up."

And muster them up he did. The gigs came sporadically, sometimes leaving Cosby wondering where his next paycheck would come from. But he remained undaunted. Both he and Roy Silver continued working diligently to further his fledgling career. While Cosby wrote and rewrote his material in an attempt to hone it, his manager mapped out strategies and searched for work for his client.

One of Silver's strategies was for Cosby to hire a press agent. "He had one job," Silver said of the press agent, "to plant items in columns that Bill Cosby was the first Negro ever being considered for a TV series. . . . Slowly, slowly, we got maybe seventy-five mentions, and it began to seep into people's minds in places like William Morris [one of the country's top talent agencies], and suddenly it wasn't a completely crazy notion anymore." ✿

5

"A VERY FUNNY FELLOW"

ROY SILVER KNEW early on that for Bill Cosby to become a success, the young entertainer did not need to depend on a string of one-liners, the standard fare of most comedians. And that would be especially true if Cosby was ever going to break into television. Even though many of the television series in the 1960s were comedies, the entertainers who enjoyed a lot of success over the airwaves were not comics who sounded as though they were reciting material from a joke book. Television personalities such as Jack Benny, Jackie Gleason, and Red Skelton did not just tell funny jokes. There was another reason for their success: They were funny *people*.

Cosby had little trouble in determining what type of a comedian he had become. "I don't think I could write an out and out joke if my life depended on it," he said. "Practically all my bits deal with my childhood days back in Philly where the important thing on the block was how far you could throw a football. . . . I think what people like most about my stories is that they can identify. I had a man once stop me and say, 'Hey, you know that story you tell about street football and you'd cut behind a car? Well . . . I used to do the same thing in the country, but I used a cow!' "

"I see things funny," Cosby said, "and I talk about the way I see them. I try to project a family atmosphere—intimate, like sharing a joke with your friends or relatives in your home."

53

According to comedian Steve Allen, "The means by which [Cosby] works his particular magic can be stated simply enough. First, he is eminently likeable. He establishes such rapport during his first few seconds onstage that everything else he does is enormously facilitated. . . . Cosby almost immediately achieves the relaxation of his audience." Allen added that "some very successful comedians leave an audience ill at ease. Jerry Lewis, Jack Carter, and Don Rickles are aggressive, dominating. Lenny Bruce and Mort Sahl have made audiences squirm by their irreverence and daring. But Cosby has such confidence in his own abilities that he is able to avoid the compulsion that drives most comedians to get that first big laugh immediately."

As Cosby proceeded to abandon racial humor in favor of everyday situations that people could relate to, he concentrated on writing comedy monologues. "Noah and the Ark" was one of his most successful early routines. The monologue featured Cosby's depiction of a biblical patriarch who refuses to believe that God has singled him out to build an ark.

> "Noah."
> "Who is that?"
> "It's the Lord, Noah."
> "Ri-ight. . ."
> "I want you to build an ark. . . . I'm gonna make it rain for four thousand days and drown [the earth]."
> "Ri-ight. Listen, do this and you'll save water. Let it rain for forty days and forty nights and wait for the sewers to back up."
> "Ri-ight!"

Cosby's ability to conceive a monologue such as "Noah and the Ark," which did not have anything to do with his past experiences in North Philadelphia, was clearly a sign that he was becoming more inventive.

By 1963, things were beginning to come together for Cosby. He began playing at better venues, including both the Shadows and the Shoreham Hotel in Washington, D.C. His salary increased, sometimes to as much as $500 a week, and the offers to perform arrived with greater frequency.

In spite of the mounting applause for his talents, Cosby would look back on the early 1960s with some embarrassment. "I have a tape of the first concert I ever gave," he said in 1982. "I was so bad that I'll never let anybody else hear it. But I learned. Anybody can learn. Once you show the basic talent, comedy can be taught, just like brain surgery, or how to be a better baseball player."

Cosby's ability to learn soon paid off handsomely. Thanks to Silver's efforts, an executive at Warner Bros. agreed to explore the possibility of putting together a record deal for Cosby. Toward the end of 1963, the company signed him for $2,500. Shortly thereafter, he recorded his first comedy album, *Bill Cosby Is a Very Funny Fellow . . . Right!*, while performing at the Bitter End in Greenwich Village. In addition to the "Noah" monologue, the album offered other skewed Cosby observations about everyday life. Not one cut was based on his childhood experiences.

"Bill Cosby has a wonderful, cockeyed, fresh sense of humor," comedian Allan Sherman, who coproduced the album with Roy Silver, wrote in the back-cover notes. "He is so good that what he has is more than talent; he has the gift of comedy. He has something that makes you feel delight when you're with him."

The public seemed to agree with Sherman's assessment. The album rose rapidly on the best-seller charts and reached number 21—quite an accomplishment for any comedy record, let alone one by a virtually unknown performer. All told, it stayed on the charts for an astounding 122 weeks. The record subsequently earned Cosby a Grammy Award nomination for Best Comedy Album of the Year.

Nineteen sixty-three proved to be a turning point in Cosby's life in more ways than one. It was also the year he met Camille Hanks, a stunningly beautiful 19-year-old psychology major at the University of Maryland. Cosby, then 26, was in Washington, D.C., for an engagement at the Shadows.

"We had a mutual friend," Camille recalled, "who asked me if I would go out on a blind date with Bill and I refused. Growing up as I did, I believed in everything awful I'd ever heard about show business people and I was afraid. But later someone brought Bill to my bowling class and he sat back, cutting up as usual. He didn't look at all like the ogre I'd expected, so we went out. The second week I knew him he asked me to marry him. Three months later I said yes."

The loving couple soon found out, however, that their relationship was not destined to go smoothly at first. "On that first visit I was making $450 a week," Cosby said, "and when I went back I was making $750. Her mother was suspicious about that. She didn't see how I could be making so much money. Anyway, she didn't want any entertainer running away with her daughter."

Determined to protect Camille, the Hankses sent her to live with relatives in Virginia, and the engagement with Cosby was broken. "I could understand her mother's feelings," he admitted, "but I had feelings of my own." Apparently, such feelings overrode her parents' fears, and the Hankses relented. On January 25, 1964, Bill Cosby married Camille Hanks in Olney, Maryland. Combining business and pleasure, they honeymooned in San Francisco, where he was playing at the Hungry I; in Lake Tahoe, where he did a stint at Harrah's; and in Los Angeles, where he was booked at the Crescendo.

"I've given up all myself to her," Cosby said of the former Camille Hanks, *whom he married in 1964. "And what happened was that I found myself falling deeper and deeper in love with her."*

By then, Cosby had become an even hotter item, demanding and getting more than $1,000 per engagement to play dates across the country. He had even managed to get himself invited onto television personality Johnny Carson's "Tonight Show." A performer could dramatically boost his or her career by appearing on the program because it was seen nightly by millions of viewers. Cosby auditioned for "The Tonight Show" three times but was rejected on each occasion.

Cosby's opportunity finally arrived when Allan Sherman was asked to fill in for Carson as host. The public responded warmly to Cosby's television debut—so warmly that he began to appear frequently as a guest on the program. Then, one day in January 1965, he was invited to serve as guest host. Cosby handled himself so well on the show that he was asked to fill this role again and again. All told, he served as guest host on "The Tonight Show" more than 70 times.

A familiar scene on the late-night screen for nearly 20 years: television personality Johnny Carson chatting with Cosby on "The Tonight Show." Cosby made his first appearance on the program in 1964, when comedian Allan Sherman filled in for Carson as the show's host.

Cosby's second album, I Started Out as a Child, *was released in late 1964 and garnered his first Grammy Award.*

On the strength of his first record album and his initial "Tonight Show" appearance, Cosby cut a second album for Warner Bros. Recorded live at Mr. Kelly's in Chicago, *I Started Out as a Child* was released in late 1964 and wound up earning more than $1 million in sales. In addition, it earned Cosby his first Grammy Award.

I Started Out as a Child revealed Cosby developing his unique voice. Unlike the material in his first album, many of the stories in his second effort were based on his childhood experiences. *I Started Out as a Child* included a routine about street football; a monologue entitled "The Giant," which was about his father; and a story about the first kid in Cosby's neighborhood to own a pair of sneakers.

Over the years, Cosby has continued to cut comedy records. Today, he has more than 20 albums—and 5 Grammy Awards—to his credit. Several of these records feature humorous musical numbers. *Silver Throat Sings*, released in 1968, was the first of these albums. Nevertheless, it has been the records featuring his comedy routines—such as *Those of You with or Without Children, You'll Understand*, which has sold more than a million copies (an extremely rare achievement for a comedy recording)—that have enabled him to become the best-selling comedian (on records) of all time.

Cosby's success in the recording industry, his occasional appearances on television (including spots on "The Garry Moore Show" and "The Jack Paar Show" in addition to "The Tonight Show"), and a gig in Las Vegas at the Flamingo Hotel helped him achieve national notice. As a result, he had graduated from being a $5-a-night storytelling bartender to a $1,500-a-night comedian within the span of a little more than 2 years.

All of this recognition did not go unnoticed by the people in the entertainment world who are always on the lookout for hot new talent. One man in particular, producer Sheldon Leonard, had big plans for Cosby. Little did the comedian know that within months he would change forever the way the television industry portrayed black Americans on the screen. ❧

6

BREAKING NEW GROUND

Beginning IN THE 1890s, the decade in which America's film industry was born, movie studios hardly ever featured black actors and actresses on the screen. When a film contained roles that were to be filled by blacks, these parts were rarely given to black entertainers, many of whom performed in theaters and vaudeville houses across the country. Instead, the roles were assigned to white actors and actresses, whose face and hands were darkened with burned cork to make them look black.

On those occasions when black actors were allowed to appear on the screen, they had to cover their skin with burned cork, too. And, just like the whites who played blacks, they were asked to portray black characters who reinforced negative racial stereotypes.

There was no greater example of this unflattering representation of blacks than in D. W. Griffith's

Cosby became the first black to star in a television series with a white actor when he teamed up with Robert Culp in 1965 to play American secret agents in "I Spy." According to Cosby, the most challenging aspect of the show was "to do the story lines without camping—to get a laugh as an actor, not as a comedian."

1915 epic, *The Birth of a Nation*. Set in the South after the Civil War, this film glorified the white supremacist group the Ku Klux Klan while suggesting that only two types of blacks lived in the United States: loyal servants and villainous "town Negroes." Almost immediately, the film came under fire from several quarters, with the National Association for the Advancement of Colored People (NAACP), formed just six years earlier, leading the way. The organization staged an elaborate, although unsuccessful, nationwide campaign to stop the film from being shown.

By then, some blacks had already decided to take matters into their own hands and launch their own film industry. In the early 1910s, the Ebony Corporation began to make movies out of popular stories, and the Douglass Company attempted "to show the better side of Negro life" by producing war movies shortly thereafter. In 1916, even the NAACP got into the act, joining forces with the Lincoln Company to make all-black movies.

By the early 1920s, there were more than 30 independent black film production companies serving more than 700 movie houses in black communities across the United States. The best known of these companies was headed by a black midwesterner named Oscar Micheaux, who eventually produced, directed, and distributed more than 40 films that dealt with black issues. His movies starred such notable black actors as Charles Gilpin and Paul Robeson.

For the most part, few whites ever saw these low-budget productions featuring black actors. But that began to change in 1927, with the release of *The Jazz Singer*. The first film to have sound, it starred Al Jolson, a white entertainer, who played the title role in blackface. Hollywood studios subsequently sought to exploit the innovation of sound by hiring large numbers of blacks to play singers, dancers, and musicians in the background of many films.

Some blacks, among them Stepin Fetchit and Bill ("Bojangles") Robinson, were even invited to step into the foreground and take on larger parts. Fetchit, a bumbling clown who embodied the movie industry's image of blacks, became Hollywood's first black millionaire. Robinson, a tap-dance star on the vaudeville circuit, also enjoyed financial success after being paired as child star Shirley Temple's kindhearted sidekick in three films. Fetchit and Robinson's film roles continued to demean blacks, however, because they played only devoted servants and lackeys.

During the next two decades, several filmmakers attempted to cast blacks in more dignified roles. But these movies usually met with little success. Even Paul Robeson's 1933 film re-creation of his critically acclaimed stage role in *The Emperor Jones* by Eugene O'Neill received such a mixed response that he withdrew to England to make a number of films in a friendlier climate. Indeed, most black American entertainers of this period—singer and dancer Josephine Baker, above all—received much kinder treatment in Europe than they did in the United States.

Hollywood filmmakers simply felt that white America would not pay to see black movie stars. So, when Hattie McDaniel became the first black to win an Academy Award (for Best Supporting Actress for her portrayal of Scarlett O'Hara's slave in the 1939 film *Gone with the Wind*), the honor meant very little in practical terms. In the years that followed, she was offered roles only as a slave or a maid.

Hollywood finally began to cast blacks in important, multidimensional roles in the 1950s, in response to an increasing public awareness of America's racial problems. Sidney Poitier, among the first black film actors to be offered serious parts, spoke of this change on the night in 1964 when he became the

For more than half a century, black actors, including two of the best known—Stepin Fetchit (right), who played bumbling clowns and shuffling servants, and Paul Robeson (opposite page), who sought more dignified roles—were treated by Hollywood without much respect. The film and television industry's depiction of blacks as second-class citizens began to change only in the 1960s, through the efforts of Cosby and others.

first black to win an Oscar for Best Actor: "I used to go to pictures and when I saw a Negro on the screen I always left the theater feeling embarrassment and uneasiness. There was the Negro, devoid of any dignity—good maids who laughed too loudly, good butlers afraid of ghosts. I want to make motion pictures about the dignity, nobility, the magnificence of human life."

The door opened even more slowly for blacks in the television industry than it did in the movies. Although singers Ethel Waters and Nat "King" Cole each had their own television show in the 1950s, by the mid-1960s a black had yet to star in his or her own network television series. That would soon change.

In 1964, Bill Cosby was relaxing backstage after a performance at the Crescendo in Pittsburgh when he was approached by Carl Reiner. A popular comedian in his own right, Reiner produced the television comedy series "The Dick Van Dyke Show" with Sheldon Leonard. It was not long before Reiner introduced Cosby to Leonard.

At that time, Leonard was in the midst of putting together the cast and crew for "I Spy," a new television series he was producing for NBC's 1965 season. The planned show was about the exploits of two American secret agents who traveled around the world disguised as a tennis champion and his trainer. Actor Robert Culp had already been cast as the tennis pro, Kelly Robinson, when Cosby came to

Leonard's attention. According to Cosby, "Leonard thought it was time that a Negro and a white could play together in a series that did not have any racial overtones."

"I had signed Robert Culp and I looked around for his counterpart," Leonard recalled. "Then I saw Cosby on one of the variety shows and a bulb lit up—I was sure he was the man I wanted." Leonard insisted that the decision to hire Cosby was not made lightly and that it came only after conversations with network executives and an extensive investigation into Cosby's work habits and professional ethics. "From every source," Leonard said, "I learned Bill Cosby was a tireless worker, a man striving to do his best."

With little hesitation, Leonard cast Cosby to play the role of Alexander Scott, Robinson's trainer, thereby making the rising comedian the first black to star in a television series with a white actor. Just as noteworthy, the part that Cosby was asked to play did not include any racial stereotypes. His "I Spy" character was to be intelligent and resourceful, a Rhodes scholar who had mastered seven languages. Best of all, Cosby said about his proposed character, Alexander Scott did not have to defer to anyone. When somebody punched him, he could punch back.

"If anyone takes exception to this man because of his color, it would have to be a nut," Leonard said. Culp was quick to agree. "We're two guys who don't know the difference between a colored and a white man," he said. Each hour-long episode of the show proved his point. In "I Spy," Cosby's and Culp's characters carry on an extremely amiable relationship.

Not everything went smoothly at first, however. Cosby has readily admitted that when "I Spy" initially went into production, his acting left much to

Producer Sheldon Leonard (right) directs Cosby and a young Chinese actor during the filming of an "I Spy" episode in Hong Kong. "When I was hired to do 'I Spy' in 1964," Cosby said, "I was so bad in the first segment that I was an embarrassment even to myself. And the word came down from one of the executives: Get rid of Cosby."

be desired. His movements were too stiff; he needed to become more at ease in front of the camera, and that was a major challenge. "I had to learn," Cosby said, "that the face speaks, the muscles of your neck, your hands, your eyebrows all act."

Cosby's early work was so poor, in fact, that he was almost fired from the show. He mumbled his dialogue and did not listen to the other actors' words, which prevented him from reacting properly to their lines. "Storytelling was one thing," he said, "but playing a definite character . . ."

"Bill was a rank beginner at acting," Culp acknowledged. "After the network executives viewed

After winning his third consecutive Emmy Award for Outstanding Performance by an Actor in a Leading Role in a Dramatic Series, Cosby poses backstage at the 1968 Emmy Awards telecast with comedians Don Adams and Lucille Ball.

our pilot, I got this phone call from 'I Spy' producer Sheldon Leonard, and he said, 'They want to fire Bill.' Culp immediately offered to pitch in and help his costar overcome his shortcomings.

Within a matter of months, Cosby managed to nail down his character. He did it in part by patterning Alexander Scott after himself. Scott, Cosby said, was "a guy who grew up in the ghetto, who went to school and took on middle-class values, who was trying to live like the white middle class. But he always knew he was black, with a real degree of black pride."

"I Spy" debuted on September 15, 1965. The show was billed as a drama, yet it possessed a wry humor, thanks in large part to Cosby, whose cool, easygoing manner softened the drama and turned "I Spy" into a hit. "At 28," *Newsweek* wrote in 1966, "Cosby has accomplished in one year what scores of Negro actors and comedians have tried to do all their lives. He has completely refurbished the television image of the Negro. He is not the stereotyped, white-toothed Negro boy with a sense of good rhythm. He is a human being, and a funnier, hipper human being than anyone around him."

Cosby went on to win an Emmy Award in the spring of 1966 for his performance in the show. As it turned out, he was cited for Outstanding Performance by an Actor in a Leading Role in a Dramatic Series in each of the three years that "I Spy" was on television. On his way to winning these Emmys, he beat out such seasoned veterans as Richard Crenna, David Janssen, David McCallum, and his acting coach and friend, Robert Culp.

At times, Cosby admitted to feeling guilty about being on the series. He was aware that many black actors were unemployed, whereas he could easily pull down tens of thousands of dollars by working his comedy routine at the resort hotels in Nevada, which

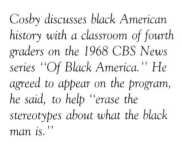

Cosby discusses black American history with a classroom of fourth graders on the 1968 CBS News series "Of Black America." He agreed to appear on the program, he said, to help "erase the stereotypes about what the black man is."

he did whenever his schedule permitted. He could also earn smaller, although by no means paltry, paychecks by playing nightclubs and college campuses across the country.

Yet the benefits of working on "I Spy" made up for any misgivings he may have had from time to time. Although the schedule for shooting the show may have been hectic, it beat traveling all over the country to perform one-night stands and weekend gigs. Leonard had decided to film the series in exotic locations rather than confine it to the sets in a Hollywood back lot. So, playing the role of Alexander Scott gave Cosby the chance to travel to cities in Europe and Asia.

Cosby's family often joined him on these foreign trips. "I couldn't travel half as happily without my family," he said at the time, "and that certainly includes Mom. It's one of the few luxuries that's really important to me. I know there's no way to repay her for being the kind of a mother she's been, but I can at least give her a few things now and a chance to see some of the world." By this time, Bill and Camille Cosby's family also included two daughters: Erika Ranee and Erinn Charlene. In the years that followed, the Cosbys would have two more daughters, Evin Harrah and Ensa Camille, and one son, Ennis William. (According to Cosby, all of his children's first names begin with an *E* because "it's a way of reminding them each day throughout their lives that *E* stands for excellence.")

Through all the travel and hard work, Cosby remained philosophical about his ground-breaking role on the show. "I'm no Show Biz buff," he said. "I wasn't born in a trunk. In five years I plan to get out. If I'm careful, I'll have enough money to quit and go back to college." The University of Massachusetts was one place he was considering attending. "I'd like to become a teacher," he added, "a physical education teacher, probably. That's what I planned to do originally. I think I have a talent for teaching; it's not so different from entertaining really, and if teaching's a thing you can do, it's something you *should* be doing."

As things turned out, Cosby did become a teacher . . . in his very own television show. ❧

7

BRANCHING OUT

⟪◆⟫

I N MARCH 1968, while he was appearing in his third season on "I Spy," Bill Cosby starred in his first television special. It was basically a one-man comedy show in which he drew upon his childhood experiences. Rave reviews for the program paved the way for more television appearances, which included another variety special the following year and a third one in 1970.

By then, NBC had canceled "I Spy." Shortly after the show's initial success, a number of other programs that featured secret agents entered the television market and captured a large share of "I Spy"'s audience. As a result, the show went off the air in September 1968.

Cosby was still riding the crest of his three Emmy wins, though, so it was not difficult for NBC executives to convince him to strike again while he was hot. This time, however, he would not be sharing the billing with another actor, black *or* white. Bill Cosby would be the show's lone star.

In September 1969, exactly one year after "I Spy" ended, his second television series, "The Bill Cosby Show," made its debut. Cosby was cast as Chet Kincaid, a likable middle-class physical education teacher. The story line of each episode revolved

Cosby wears a T-shirt bearing the image and favorite phrase of one of his most popular creations, Fat Albert, the star of the Saturday morning cartoon show "Fat Albert and the Cosby Kids."

75

around his daily interactions with students, family members, and friends.

The program was by no means a zany situation comedy. "The Bill Cosby Show," its star explained, was about "a human being. He makes mistakes, gets into trouble, and reflects quite frequently on the human condition."

As was the case with "I Spy," "The Bill Cosby Show" was not easy to categorize. It did not attempt to capture a slice of black ghetto life and deal with penetrating racial issues. Nor did it present Kincaid as a goody-two-shoes who had the right answer for every imaginable problem. Instead, Cosby's character was a real person. As Cosby described it, "He'll put his feet up on the desk, jump on the trampoline with his shoes on, and frequently act out of selfish motives." In short, Chet Kincaid was not like most black characters who appeared on television.

Just like Diahann Carroll, who in 1968 became the first black actress to star in her own television series (in "Julia"), Cosby received criticism for presenting a comedy that showed a black person who acted just like whites did. "I'm aware that the show will have a negative meaning for people who are really militant about any story with a black person in it, black viewers included," he said at the time. "But you can still pick a guy's pocket while he's laughing, and that's what I hope to do."

Indeed, Cosby often placed his character in a position that had him trying to teach a lesson to others. In one episode, an environmentally conscious Kincaid attempted to save a tree that had to be destroyed so a new building could be constructed. Another episode showed him teaching one of the players on the school's football team to be humble in victory and gracious in defeat. In that episode, however, Cosby's character did not practice what he preached. Participating in a handball tournament,

Cosby stars as physical education teacher Chet Kincaid in "The Bill Cosby Show." A forerunner of "The Cosby Show," his second television series featured slice-of-life stories.

A group of youngsters in his native Philadelphia help Cosby film part of his first comedy special. Over the years, he has appeared in numerous television programs, ranging from comedy specials to dramatic movies, in addition to his television series.

Kincaid tried a number of cheap tricks to come in first place, only to lose to someone who attempted the same tactics.

Unfortunately for Cosby, his second series did not come up a big winner, either. "The Bill Cosby Show" became the top-rated new program of 1969–70 and ended the season as the 11th-most-watched show overall. But the number of viewers fell off considerably the following season, and NBC canceled the series in the summer of 1971.

Cosby was not at a loss for things to do; he made that clear by keeping himself busy with other projects while making "The Bill Cosby Show." In 1970, he taught a weekly class about television at the University of Southern California. That same year, he was asked to serve as host of both the Grammy Awards and the Emmy Awards telecasts. In 1971, he hosted a television special aimed at youngsters, "Bill Cosby Talks with Children About Drugs."

And Cosby still packed them in wherever he performed his stand-up comedy act. Clearly, the cancellation of his second series was not a sign that he had lost favor with the American public. All that remained for him was to find the right kind of program to display his talents to their fullest.

Cosby tried a few different routes. In 1971, he made the first of his many guest appearances on public television's "Electric Company," a program designed to help youngsters improve their reading skills. He was subsequently featured on another children's show, the critically acclaimed "Wake Up with Captain Kangaroo," appearing daily in five-minute segments aimed at a preschool audience. His efforts helped the show win the Outstanding Children's Program Award at the 1981 International Film and Television Festival.

Cosby had laid the groundwork for his involvement in children's television back in November 1968, when NBC had aired "Hey, Hey—It's Fat Albert," an animated half-hour show that brought to life Cosby's crowd of pals from his Philadelphia boyhood. In September 1972, Fat Albert and his friends became a fixture in Saturday morning television's cartoon lineup on "Fat Albert and the Cosby Kids." (The name of the show was changed in 1979 to "The New Fat Albert Show.")

"The way I see the show," Cosby said before the first episode of the cartoon was telecast, "it will be so casual in its teaching they'll never know they're being taught. It will have Fat Albert and Old Weird Harold and those other characters I made up, but they will get themselves involved in things like mathematical equations and what geometry is all about and why." Much to Cosby's delight, Fat Albert and his friends were warmly received by children and adults alike. With Cosby himself appearing on the program, the cartoon wound up winning several educational awards, including the 1973 Children's Theater Association Seal of Excellence.

Cosby himself returned to prime-time programming in February 1972, when he starred in the touching made-for-television movie "To All My Friends on Shore." According to television critic Cecil Smith, the movie "reaches inside you and pulls at you with such force that time must pass after you see it before you can go on with your life and take up other things again." Cosby not only helped develop the story, which was about a dreamer (played by Cosby) who learns to live for the present after discovering that his son is dying from sickle-cell anemia, but he also wrote the musical score.

Cosby's next prime-time venture was the launching of his third series, "The New Bill Cosby Show." Aired in September 1972 on a different network (CBS) than the one that had carried his past shows, the program featured a variety format. The public's response was hardly overwhelming, however. This new effort fared even worse than its predecessors and was axed after its first season.

Convinced that a variety format would work for him, Cosby gave it one more try. "Cos" premiered on ABC in September 1976. The show was a resounding disaster, barely lasting six weeks before the network canceled it.

Although Cosby's television career seemed to be at a standstill, his life off camera was progressing nicely. In 1971, almost 10 years after he had dropped out of Temple University, he felt the time had come to get the degree that had eluded him earlier. Accordingly, he pulled up his roots and moved his family from California to an area near Amherst,

Massachusetts, where he bought 286 acres and restored a 16-room 19th-century clapboard farmhouse to serve as his family's main home. At the nearby University of Massachusetts, he worked toward rounding out his education. His coursework was subsequently approved by Temple's School of Communications, which conferred on him a bachelor of arts degree.

In spite of his busy schedule, Cosby continued his studies at the University of Massachusetts over the next few years. First, he received a master's degree in education. Then, in May 1976, just 2 months prior to his 39th birthday, he earned a doctorate in education, thereby becoming Dr. William H. Cosby (the name that is proudly displayed in the credits of "The Cosby Show"). On the day that he received this prestigious degree, Cosby was accompanied to the graduation ceremonies by a group of elated family

Cosby addresses a group of youngsters on the educational television series "The Electric Company." The half-hour program, which debuted in 1971, was designed to help children improve their reading skills.

members and friends. None of them was more ecstatic than his mother. "Mom just went crazy today," Cosby said later in the day. "She used to say, 'Education's a must.' If she was dead, she would have gotten up to come here today."

As if all these accomplishments were not enough, Cosby managed to find the time to embark on still another career path: acting in feature films. His first effort, *Man and Boy*, which Cosby's own company released in 1972, was a western set in the days after the Civil War. Cosby played the role of Caleb, a former slave trying to eke out a living on a meager tract of land. When his family's workhorse is stolen, Caleb and his son set out on an odyssey to find the animal.

Critics found much to recommend in this story about a black cowboy. One reviewer cited the film for being "believable and fresh with no cardboard heroes." The *New York Times* called *Man and Boy*

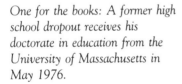

One for the books: A former high school dropout receives his doctorate in education from the University of Massachusetts in May 1976.

"wonderfully provocative" and said that "it puts Mr. Cosby on first base in screen drama." Nevertheless, the film failed to garner a large viewing audience.

Unfortunately for Cosby, he also failed to connect for a hit his next time up. Teaming with Robert Culp once again, he played a private eye trying to recover nearly half a million dollars in stolen money in the action-packed 1972 film *Hickey and Boggs*. But the reunion of the "I Spy" stars could not salvage this unconvincing movie, and it fared poorly at the box office.

Suddenly, it seemed that Cosby was unable to sustain a hit either on television or in the movies. That would all change with his next film, which would allow Cosby the opportunity to be his typical self and make people laugh. ✦

Cosby fills in as guest host of "The Tonight Show," interviewing former "I Spy" costar Robert Culp in August 1981. Cosby first hosted the popular late-night program in January 1965.

8

THE KING OF COMEDY

I N THE LATE 1960s and early 1970s, a new film genre emerged in Hollywood: the black exploitation movie. Fast paced and action packed, these films featured Jim Brown, Pam Grier, Richard Roundtree, and other black actors and actresses venting their anger on double-crossing drug dealers, petty criminals, and assorted low-life characters. Sometimes called blaxploitation movies, these films were also noisy and violent and filled with a charged-up hatred of the white establishment. Bill Cosby had no interest in making this type of film, no matter how profitable it was.

Nor did his friend Sidney Poitier. "My understanding of the film business," said the Academy Award–winning actor, "told me that the producers were not interested in much beyond the buck. Past the point where that buck stopped, there wasn't a genuine interest in the black audience." In response, Poitier began to develop his own film projects.

One of them was *Uptown Saturday Night*, a comedy that the entire family could enjoy. Poitier intended the film to uplift blacks rather than exploit them, a point that quickly caught Cosby's attention. He joined the project along with singer and actor

A playful Cosby mugs for the audience at New York City's prestigious Radio City Music Hall. He has performed his unique brand of stand-up comedy act in all sorts of venues, including on Broadway, where he costarred with entertainer Sammy Davis, Jr., in a two-man show in 1983.

85

Harry Belafonte. Comedians Richard Pryor and Flip Wilson rounded out the star-studded cast.

Released in 1974, *Uptown Saturday Night* became a wildly successful crossover film, a smash hit with both black and white audiences. "Full of good humor," the *New York Times* raved about the movie, which presented Cosby and Poitier as two friends who track down a winning lottery ticket after it is stolen from them by gangsters. Along the way, the duo becomes involved in a series of hilarious misadventures.

"The success of *Uptown Saturday Night* told me that black people wanted to laugh at themselves and have," Poitier said. "They were weary of being represented on the local screen by pimps, hustlers, prostitutes, private detectives, violence, macho men and dirty words." Indeed, the reaction to the film was so positive that it led to two similar projects, *Let's Do It Again* (1975) and *A Piece of the Action*. Like *Uptown Saturday Night*, both of these movies became huge hits.

Even though he had these films to his credit, Cosby failed to become one of Hollywood's top box-office draws. Farfetched plots and weak scripts undermined nearly all the movies he subsequently made without Poitier. The lone exception was *Bill Cosby, Himself* (1983), a concert film written and directed by Cosby. "I just haven't been able to put together the kind of show where the public will say, 'Hey, let's watch!'" he said. "It's as simple as that."

Mother, Juggs and Speed, the first of these movies, was released in 1976; Raquel Welch and Harvey Keitel costarred in this hip comedy about a group of ambulance paramedics. Two years later, Cosby took on the role of Dr. Willis Panama in the Neil Simon comedy *California Suite*. Next, he turned to children's entertainment and appeared as one of the Devil's henchmen in the 1981 Walt Disney film *The Devil and Max Devlin*.

Cosby ponders the problem of being a ghost in the 1989 film Ghost Dad. *Accepting the role gave him the opportunity to work once more with director Sidney Poitier.*

READ

Bill Cosby
and friends
for America's
Libraries

A longtime advocate of education, Cosby is featured in an advertisement to promote reading. "I think there's a lot to be said," he observed, "for fighting at the blackboard, with a piece of chalk as a weapon."

Cosby played a secret agent in his subsequent big-screen effort, *Leonard Part 6* (1987). Extremely unsatisfied with the project, he attempted to dissociate himself from the film, which flopped. He expected his fortunes to rise with his next movie, *Ghost Dad* (1989), but as it turned out, not even Sidney Poitier, who was the director, could help revive Cosby's flagging movie career.

Cosby fared much better at reaching a large audience through his literary output. He began his career as an author with *The Wit and Wisdom of Fat Albert* (1973) and *Fat Albert's Survival Kit* (1975), two books about his beloved childhood character. Cosby's next published work was *Bill Cosby's Personal Guide to Power Tennis; or Don't Lower the Lob, Raise the Net* (1975), a humorous look at one of his favorite sports.

Cosby did not write another book for more than a decade. But when he did so in 1986, he instantly became a phenomenon in the publishing world. Riding the coattails of "The Cosby Show," which was firmly established by then as television's number one program, *Fatherhood*, his collection of anecdotes and observations about being a dad, spent more than a year on the best-seller list, with almost 3 million copies sold in hardcover.

Fatherhood's smashing success prompted Cosby to write a second memoir, *Time Flies*. Released one year after *Fatherhood*—just in time to honor his 50th birthday—*Time Flies* offered the comedian's views on growing older. "Aging is no laughing matter," noted Alvin Poussaint, "but *Time Flies* will change all that."

After Cosby added *Love and Marriage*, a memoir about relationships, to his canon in 1989, one observer noted, "Perhaps no performer in history has chronicled his life cycle so thoroughly, or so publicly, as Bill Cosby. Certainly no one has been so successful at it."

Indeed, most projects that Cosby has touched during the past decade have turned to gold. According to *Time* magazine, he "has parlayed his TV success into a multimedia empire that seems to grow like the tall tales the young stand-up comic once spun out of his Philadelphia childhood." This far-reaching empire includes not only "The Cosby Show," his best-selling books and records, his Hollywood movies, and his standing-room-only stand-up

comedy performances but a top-selling concert video, *Bill Cosby: 49.*

The emergence of this empire, which some observers have called Cosby, Inc., unofficially dates back to 1974, when Jell-O hired him to advertise Jell-O pudding in a series of television commercials. In the years since then, Cosby has served as a spokesman for Coca-Cola, Dutch Masters, the Ford Motor Company, E. F. Hutton, Kodak, and Texas

Seeking to spur his alma mater on to victory, Cosby borrows a horn and joins the student band moments before tip-off of a game between Temple University and Duke University in 1988.

Instruments. According to advertising executives, Cosby's ability to communicate with children and adults of all races makes him the ideal pitchman. "Our ratings polls show that he is extremely credible," a Coca-Cola executive said in explaining why Cosby is one of America's top commercial salesmen.

Nowadays, much of Cosby's credibility can be attributed to the dual image of calm authority and compassion that he allows Cliff Huxtable to project on "The Cosby Show." By all accounts, Dr. Huxtable's expressions of love and trust are deeply rooted in Cosby's own personal life, the foundation of which is his rock-steady marriage. Every year, to make a public showing of his tremendous affection for Camille, he holds an I Love My Wife party attended by a large gathering of family members and friends (among the guests have been basketball great Julius Erving and psychologist Kenneth Clarke).

For the most part, though, Cosby has been fiercely protective of his family and has tried to keep details of their life together private. "I've got two attitudes on that subject," he said. "One, I don't get into personal specifics, because I love them and want to protect them. . . . On the other hand, talking about kids is part of my business, and part of how I relate to other kids, professionally and personally."

Cosby's insistence on being a family man is a major reason why "The Cosby Show" has been produced in Brooklyn rather than across the continent in Hollywood, where most television series are taped. After wrapping up the production of an episode, he has usually commuted to his house in Massachusetts so he can spend the weekend with his wife and kids in their own home. "I think it's the little things that count when you're a daddy," Cosby explained. "Like taking your little girl for ice cream. First you have to teach her about the concept of gravity. I can't tell you how many ice creams I've had to pick up off the floor."

Cosby has made a point of keeping his children's feet firmly planted on the ground, cautioning them against taking their family's affluence for granted. "I tell them that I'm going to leave them an awful lot of money," he said, "but that nobody is getting anything unless they have a formal education and can understand what to do with that money."

And it is an extraordinary amount of money, indeed. During the past several years, the former high school dropout from Philadelphia has earned more money than any other entertainer in the world, making tens of millions of dollars annually from his various endeavors. In 1986, for example, Cosby netted $22 million by selling to superstation WWOR the right to rerun past episodes of "The Cosby Show" for the next 3½ years.

Eager to put this money to good use, Cosby and his wife created quite a stir in November 1988 by announcing that they were giving $20 million to Spelman College, the elite black women's college in Atlanta. "Mrs. Cosby and I have been blessed because I found a vein of gold in the side of the mountain," he said at the time. Thereafter, he modestly refused to discuss their gift, which was the largest contribution ever made to a black college.

Cosby, it seems, has refused to let his success go to his head. Nor has he been willing to rest on his past achievements. He continues to support many causes, speaks out against drug use and teenage pregnancy, and busies himself with new projects. One of them, he said, is "a new TV series about a couple in their fifties who break up after 29 years of marriage. The series will be called 'The Road Back.' I want to write funny about a 50-year-old woman who has to take on jobs she does not want to in order to keep going. This'll be a sitcom, not a soap. I want to show someone who can keep on growing, without bitterness." He has also been developing "Black Collar," a show that deals with a West Virginia

Unspoiled by the success of his vast multimedia empire, Cosby and his wife, Camille, have made the largest contribution ever to a black school—a $20 million gift to Spelman College, the elite black women's college in Atlanta.

coal-mining community, and he has been writing a book.

Another of Cosby's current projects has him serving as producer, co-composer, and part-time percussionist on a series of albums for the Verve/ Polygram label. A longtime jazz lover, he has dedicated himself to promoting the nation's first popular black art form. He has hosted the annual Playboy Jazz Festival and has peppered "The Cosby Show" with guest appearances by music legends such as Joe Williams, B. B. King, Nancy Wilson, Dizzy Gillespie, and Lena Horne.

On an entirely different front, Cosby has been a staunch supporter of the Philadelphia-based Penn Relays, perhaps the nation's most prestigious amateur track meet. He has also been attempting to put together a competive car-racing team manned by blacks—a group that he hopes can win the Indianapolis 500. As in everything else he now does, Cosby wants to project a positive view of black Americans. "This country is complex and difficult to read," he said in 1989. "There are subtle ways we see certain negatives reinforced for minorities and young people."

A perfect example, Cosby explained, was when one critic of "The Cosby Show" complained that it was unrealistic: "'The problem is that they talk about college too much, which puts too much pressure on the kids.' What do you think that reinforces?" Cosby countered. "Is it that difficult for you to set a goal for yourself, or solve a math problem? When's the last time we totally crumbled because we set a goal and couldn't make it?"

Cosby feels that if he can use his celebrity to change things for the better, as he has tried to do through "The Cosby Show," then he will attempt just that. "It may seem like I'm an authority," he notes, "because my skin color gives me the mark of the victim. But that's not a true label." It has been that way with him ever since his childhood days. As long as there is an audience that will pay attention to his subtle lessons on life, all of which are served up with a generous portion of humor, Bill Cosby cannot resist the temptation to keep on teaching.

APPENDIX:
A BILL COSBY MISCELLANY

ALBUMS

1963	*Bill Cosby Is a Very Funny Fellow . . . Right!*
1964	*I Started Out as a Child*
1965	*Why Is There Air?*
1966	*Wonderfulness*
1967	*Revenge*
1968	*To Russell, My Brother, Whom I Slept With; 200 MPH; Silver Throat Sings*
1969	*It's True! It's True!; 8:15 12:15; Bill Cosby: Sports; The Best of Bill Cosby; Hooray for the Salvation Army Band*
1970	*Live at Madison Square Garden; More of the Best of Bill Cosby*
1971	*When I Was a Kid; Bill Cosby Talks to Kids About Drugs*
1972	*For Adults Only; Inside the Mind of Bill Cosby; Bill Cosby Presents Badfoot Brown and the Bunions Bradford Funeral and Marching Band*
1973	*Fat Albert; Bill*
1974	*At Last Bill Cosby Really Sings*
1976	*Bill Cosby Is Not Himself These Days, Rat Own, Rat Own, Rat Own*
1977	*My Father Confused Me, What Must I Do?; Disco Bill*
1978	*Bill's Best Friend*
1983	*Bill Cosby, Himself*
1987	*Those of You With or Without Children*
1990	*Where You Lay Your Head*

BOOKS

1973	*The Wit and Wisdom of Fat Albert*
1975	*Fat Albert's Survival Kit; Bill Cosby's Personal Guide to Power Tennis*
1986	*Fatherhood*
1987	*Time Flies*
1989	*Love and Marriage*

FILMS

1972	*Man and Boy; Hickey and Boggs*
1974	*Uptown Saturday Night*
1975	*Let's Do It Again*
1976	*Mother, Juggs and Speed*
1977	*A Piece of the Action*
1978	*California Suite*
1981	*The Devil and Max Devlin*
1983	*Bill Cosby, Himself*
1987	*Leonard Part 6*
1989	*Ghost Dad*

TELEVISION SERIES

1965–68	"I Spy"
1969–71	"The Bill Cosby Show"
1971–76	"The Electric Company"
1972–78	"Fat Albert and the Cosby Kids"
1972–73	"The New Bill Cosby Show"
1976	"Cos"
1984–	"The Cosby Show"

CHRONOLOGY

1937   Born William Henry Cosby, Jr., on July 12 in Philadelphia, Pennsylvania

1956   Drops out of high school and joins the U.S. Navy; becomes a physical therapist

1959   Passes a high school equivalency exam

1960   Leaves the U.S. Navy

1961   Enrolls at Temple University

1962   Begins career as a stand-up comic; leaves Temple University

1963   Records first comedy album, *Bill Cosby Is a Very Funny Fellow . . . Right!*

1964   Marries Camille Hanks; makes first appearance on "The Tonight Show"

1965   Serves for the first time as guest host on "The Tonight Show"; wins first Grammy Award (for *I Started Out as a Child*); debuts in "I Spy" and becomes the first black to star in television in a dramatic series

1966   Wins first Emmy Award

1969   Debuts in "The Bill Cosby Show"

1971   Makes first appearance on "The Electric Company"

1972   Appears in first television movie, *To All My Friends on Shore,* and first feature film, *Man and Boy;* cartoon series, "Fat Albert and the Cosby Kids," and "The New Bill Cosby Show" debut

1976   Cosby receives a doctorate in education from the University of Massachusetts; debuts in "Cos"

1983   Appears in first concert film, *Bill Cosby, Himself*

1984   Debuts in "The Cosby Show"

1986   Publishes first best-seller, *Fatherhood*

1988   Donates $20 million to Spelman College

FURTHER READING

Adams, Barbara Johnston. *The Picture Life of Bill Cosby.* New York: Watts, 1986.

Cosby, Bill. *Fatherhood.* New York: Doubleday, 1986.

———. *Love and Marriage.* New York: Doubleday, 1989.

———. *Time Flies.* New York: Doubleday, 1987.

Haskins, Jim. *Bill Cosby: America's Most Famous Father.* Houston: Walker, 1988.

Hill, George H. *Bill Cosby: In Our Living Room for Twenty Years.* Los Angeles: Daystar, 1986.

Johnson, Robert. *Bill Cosby: In Words and Pictures.* Chicago: Johnson, 1986.

Null, Gary. *Black Hollywood: The Black Performers in Motion Pictures.* Secaucus, NJ: Citadel, 1975.

Smith, Ronald L. *Cosby.* New York: St. Martin's Press, 1986.

Woods, Harold, and Geraldine Woods. *Bill Cosby: Making America Laugh and Learn.* Minneapolis: Dillon, 1983.

INDEX

Allen, Steve, 54
Allen, Woody, 44
Amateur Athletics Union, 39
Amherst, Massachusetts, 81

Baker, Josephine, 65
Belafonte, Harry, 86
Benny, Jack, 53
Bethesda Naval Hospital, 37
Bill Cosby: 49, 91
Bill Cosby, Himself, 86
Bill Cosby Is a Very Funny Fellow . . . Right!, 55
"Bill Cosby Show, The," 75, 76, 78
Bill Cosby's Personal Guide to Power Tennis; or Don't Lower the Lob, Raise the Net, 89
"Bill Cosby Talks with Children About Drugs," 79
Birth of a Nation, The, 64
Bitter End, 55
"Black Collar," 93–94
Bledsoe, Tempestt, 14
Bonet, Lisa, 14
Brown, Jim, 85
Bruce, Lenny, 48, 54

California Suite, 86
Cambridge, Godfrey, 46
Carroll, Diahann, 76
Carsey, Marcy, 12
Carson, Johnny, 58
Carter, Jack, 54
CEBA (Communications Excellence to Black Audiences) Award, 19
Cellar, 43, 44
Central High School, 34
Cole, Nat "King," 67
"Cos," 80

Cosby, Anna Pearl (mother), 21, 23, 26, 27, 73, 82
Cosby, Camille Hanks (wife), 12, 15, 56, 73, 92
Cosby, Ennis William (son), 73
Cosby, Ensa Camille (daughter), 73
Cosby, Erika Ranee (daughter), 73
Cosby, Erinn Charlene (daughter), 73
Cosby, Evin Harrah (daughter), 73
Cosby, James (brother), 21, 23
Cosby, Robert (brother), 21, 27
Cosby, Russell (brother), 21, 27
"Cosby Show, The," 11, 13, 15, 16, 18, 27, 28, 81, 89, 90, 92, 94, 95
Cosby, William (father), 21, 23, 28
Cosby, William Henry (Bill)
  attitudes about blacks on television, 11, 18, 19
  awards, 19, 60, 61, 71
  childhood, 21–36
  college years, 39
  comedy albums, 55, 60, 61
  as commercial spokesman, 90, 91
  early years as stand-up comic, 43–61
  education, 38, 39, 81–82
  first comedy album, 55
  first job as comedian, 43
  first television appearance, 59
  marries Camille Hanks, 56
  navy experience, 37, 38
  television roles, 11, 68, 70, 72, 74, 75, 76, 78, 92
  wins athletic scholarship, 39

Crenna, Richard, 71
Crescendo, 56, 67
Culp, Robert, 15, 67, 68, 70, 71, 83

Davis, Sammy, Jr., 15
Devil and Max Devlin, The, 86
"Dick Van Dyke Show, The," 67
"Different World, A," 19
Douglass Company, 64
Dylan, Bob, 46

Ebony Corporation, 64
"Electric Company, The," 79
Emmy Awards, 19, 71, 75, 79
Emperor Jones, The (O'Neill), 65

"Fat Albert and the Cosby Kids," 79
Fat Albert's Survival Kit, 89
Fatherhood, 28, 29
Fetchit, Stepin, 65
Forchic, Mary, 29, 31–33
Franklin Field, 41

Gardner, Paul, 49
"Garry Moore Show, The," 61
Gaslight, 44, 46, 49
Gate of Horn, 49
Germantown High School, 36
Ghost Dad, 89
Gillespie, Dizzy, 94
Gilpin, Charles, 64
Gleason, Jackie, 53
Golden Globe Award, 19
Gone with the Wind, 65
Grammy Awards, 56, 60, 79
Greenwich Village, 44, 48, 55
Gregory, Dick, 46
Grier, Pam, 85
Griffith, D. W., 63

Guantánamo Bay, Cuba, 37

"Hey, Hey—It's Fat Albert," 79
Hickey and Boggs, 83
Hood, Clarence, 46
Horne, Lena, 94
Humanitas Award, 19
Hungry I, 56

International Film and Television Festival, 1981, 79
"I Spy," 68, 70–72, 75, 76, 83
I Started Out as a Child, 60, 61

"Jack Paar Show, The," 61
Janssen, David, 71
Jazz Singer, The, 64
Johnson, Joe, 27
Jolson, Al, 64
"Julia," 76

Keitel, Harvey, 86
King, B. B., 94
Kistlinger, Anita, 16

Leonard, Sheldon, 61, 67, 68, 70, 72
Leonard Part 6, 89
Let's Do It Again, 86
Lewis, Jerry, 54
Lincoln Company, 64
Los Angeles Times, 25
Love and Marriage, 89

McCallum, David, 71
McDaniel, Hattie, 65
"Magnum P.I.," 13
Makris, George, 50
Man and Boy, 82
Maryland, University of, 56
Massachusetts, University of, 73, 81
Micheaux, Oscar, 64
Mr. Kelly's, 60
Mother, Juggs and Speed, 86

National Association for the Advancement of Colored People (NAACP), 64
"New Bill Cosby Show, The," 80
"New Fat Albert Show, The," 79
Newsweek magazine, 71
New York Times, 49, 82, 86

Olney, Maryland, 56

Penn Relays, 95
People's Choice Awards, 19
Philadelphia, Pennsylvania, 21, 23, 28, 31, 34, 36, 39, 41, 44, 46, 50, 54, 79, 93, 95
Philadelphia Naval Hospital, 37
Piece of the Action, A, 86
Playboy Jazz Festival, 94
Poitier, Sidney, 65, 85, 86
Police Athletic League, 31
Poussaint, Alvin, 18, 89
Pryor, Richard, 86
Pulliam, Keshia, 15

Quantico, Virginia, 37

Rashad, Phylicia, 18
Reiner, Carl, 67
Rickles, Don, 54
Rivers, Joan, 44
Robeson, Paul, 64, 65
Robinson, Bill ("Bojangles"), 65
Roundtree, Richard, 85
Russell, Samuel, 24

Sahl, Mort, 54
Selleck, Tom, 13
Shadows, 55, 56
Sherman, Allan, 55, 58
Shields, Del, 44
Shoreham Hotel, 55
Silver, Roy, 46, 50, 51, 53, 55

Silver Throat Sings, 61
Skelton, Red, 53
Smith, Cecil, 80
Southern California, University of, 78
Spelman College, 93

Tartikoff, Brandon, 12, 13
Temple University, 39, 40, 43, 50, 80, 81
Those of You With or Without Children, You'll Understand, 61
Time Flies, 89
Time magazine, 90
Tinker, Grant, 12
"To All My Friends on Shore," 80
"Tonight Show, The," 12, 58–61
Town Hall, 50
Tunnell, Emlen, 39

Underground, 43
U.S. Marine Corps, 37
U.S. Navy, 23, 37, 38
Uptown Saturday Night, 85, 86

Village Vanguard, 48

"Wake Up with Captain Kangaroo," 79
Warner, Malcolm Jamal, 14, 15
Warner Bros., 55, 60
Washington, D.C., 55, 56
Waters, Ethel, 66
Welch, Raquel, 86
Werner, Tom, 12
White, Gavin, 39, 41
William Morris (agency), 51
Williams, Joe, 94
Wilson, Flip, 86
Wilson, Nancy, 94
Wit and Wisdom of Fat Albert, The, 89

PICTURE CREDITS

SOLOMON J. HERBERT is a California-based journalist and screenwriter who has written more than 600 articles for numerous regional, national, and international publications. A native New Yorker, he is a former president of the Black Journalists Association of Southern California and a former national officer of the Congress of Racial Equality under James Farmer during the civil rights struggles of the early 1960s.

GEORGE H. HILL is a communications historian who has worked as a journalist, publicist, and producer-host of television and radio programs. He is the editor of the Los Angeles–based *TV Journal,* America's first television guide for black viewers, and is also the author of more than 15 books, including *Bill Cosby: In Our Living Rooms for Twenty Years: A Bibliography* and *Ebony Images: Black Americans and Television.* A former U.S. Air Force captain and squadron commander who holds a Ph.D. in communications, Dr. Hill has taught at Los Angeles City College and Southwest College and is currently director of the Institute of Research.

NATHAN IRVIN HUGGINS is W.E.B. Du Bois Professor of History and Director of the W.E.B. Du Bois Institute for Afro-American Research at Harvard University. He previously taught at Columbia University. Professor Huggins is the author of numerous books, including *Black Odyssey: The Afro-American Ordeal in Slavery, The Harlem Renaissance,* and *Slave and Citizen: The Life of Frederick Douglass.*